Return to Reflexivity

Pierre Bourdieu

Return to Reflexivity

Edited and introduced by
Jérôme Bourdieu and Johan Heilbron

Translated by Peter Collier

polity

Originally published in French as *Retour sur la réflexivité* © Éditions de l'EHESS, Paris, 2023

This English edition © Polity Press, 2025

Polity Press
65 Bridge Street
Cambridge CB2 1UR, UK

Polity Press
111 River Street
Hoboken, NJ 07030, USA

ISBN-13: 978-1-5095-6291-6 – hardback
ISBN-13: 978-1-5095-6292-3 – paperback

A catalogue record for this book is available from the British Library.

Library of Congress Control Number: 2024936759

Typeset in 10.25 on 14 pt Plantin MT
by Fakenham Prepress Solutions, Fakenham, Norfolk NR21 8NL
Printed and bound in Great Britain by CPI Group (UK) Ltd, Croydon

The publisher has used its best endeavours to ensure that the URLs for external websites referred to in this book are correct and active at the time of going to press. However, the publisher has no responsibility for the websites and can make no guarantee that a site will remain live or that the content is or will remain appropriate.

Every effort has been made to trace all copyright holders, but if any have been overlooked the publisher will be pleased to include any necessary credits in any subsequent reprint or edition.

For further information on Polity, visit our website:
politybooks.com

Contents

An enterprise of objectification can only be scientifically validated insofar as the subject of the objectification has been subjected to objectification in the first place.

Pierre Bourdieu, *Science of Science and Reflexivity*, trans. Richard Nice [translation adjusted] (Cambridge: Polity, 2001), p. 92.

Introduction
From epistemological vigilance to reflexivity

The demand for reflexivity, which has come to be accepted as a key principle for the human and social sciences, is one of the major contributions made by Pierre Bourdieu's work. Although all of his work bears the hallmark of a reflexive practice of research, he came to use the word itself rather late in the day. His systematic reflection on the research he was engaged in, designed to scientifically objectify his own scientific practice, was a disposition that preceded, and probably facilitated, his various intellectual innovations, including his concept of reflexivity.

Spurning the bureaucratic model of research as a mechanical application of standardized methods, Bourdieu started his career with fieldwork in wartime Algeria. These exceptional conditions were incompatible with ordinary research work, unless the researcher were to cast a reflexive gaze back onto precisely this extraordinary context, in order to register its impact on the object of research and the researcher himself. So that when Bourdieu took his native Béarn as his object of study, it paradoxically obeyed the same logic: he set out this familiar but fast-changing terrain as a mirror of Algeria, following a reflexive practice that made it possible to verify the impact of the social world on the observer. This concern to objectify and control the relationship between the observer and his object also informed the various investigations he undertook and (co)directed at the Centre de sociologie européenne (CSE), where he was recruited by his director of studies, Raymond Aron, in 1961.[1]

To understand Bourdieu's sense of reflexivity, we should go back to his early research. His first investigations were characterized by the fact that nothing came easily: none of the criteria for normal research work were satisfied. In the circumstances, the usual procedures of ethnographic or statistical research were almost impossible to apply, nor were the techniques he had acquired as a trainee philosopher much help. The context of Algeria's War of Independence, involving extreme danger and emergencies, provoked a 'permanent practical reflexivity' as a condition of survival as much as a method of research.[2] This led Bourdieu to mount a collective enterprise, with a team of investigators and researchers who drew on their diverse forms of involvement with Algerian reality. This very diversity was rich in assets, but these needed to be co-ordinated and organized, exploiting a variety of survey methods (observations, interviews, and statistical analysis) and academic resources (blurring the boundaries between anthropology, sociology, and labour economics, for example). These various scientific and managerial procedures were guided by a reflexive approach that came to typify all of his subsequent projects. This approach, which is explained explicitly in *Travail et travailleurs en Algérie* (1963),[3] was explored and elaborated on as his work progressed.

The research in Béarn, begun in 1959, appears to be an essential complement to the Algerian work then in progress. It deals with social upheavals of a completely different nature and is situated in a radically different universe, one close to Bourdieu's heart, the childhood village that he had left when he was still young to attend boarding school at the *lycée* in Pau. These studies, later collected in *The Bachelors' Ball* (2002), focus on peasant celibacy and the crisis facing peasant families.[4] They represent an acid test for these early experiments in research and provide a conclusive justification of the Algerian studies. In his self-analysis, Bourdieu describes his study of Béarn as the 'occasion and the operator of a veritable conversion':[5]

The word is, no doubt, not too strong to describe the transformation, at once intellectual and affective, that led me from the phenomenology of emotional life [*the initial theme of his thesis project*] [. . .] to a scientific practice implying a vision of the social world that was both more distanced and more realistic.[6]

In launching this twofold enterprise, Bourdieu confronted the many problems arising, not so much as technical or theoretical questions, nor even as ethical or political issues, but first and foremost in a reflexive mode. In *The Craft of Sociology* (1968), co-authored with Jean-Claude Chamboredon and Jean-Claude Passeron, this attitude is still referred to as 'epistemological vigilance'.[7] Instead of relying on logical techniques, as advocated by some philosophers of science, or on the 'methodology' of sociologists, such as Paul Lazarsfeld, it encourages the objectification of the (social) conditions of possibility of research, which depend on the generic positions of the researchers and the characteristics of their personal social trajectories. This approach requires the use of social science techniques in order to better understand and master the research in progress, its obstacles and perspectives, as well as the dispositions that researchers unwittingly deploy in their work.

This understanding of reflexivity does not imply an exercise in introspection designed to overcome some kind of lack of personal self-knowledge. Perhaps this is why Bourdieu initially preferred to speak of 'epistemological vigilance' instead of 'reflexivity', a term that he started to use more frequently only from the 1980s.[8]

The attitude of epistemological vigilance is grounded in the need to dispel the denial or ignorance of the effects of researchers' characteristics on their activity: a blindness based on the illusion of a personal talent for lucidity, which is the first obstacle to a relationship with the world conducive to sociological objectification. But even when subjecting themselves to an analysis of their unique personality and experience, researchers cannot escape the perceptual biases that are social. It is only by trying to take account of all the social mechanisms that construct the human person, including their belief in their uniqueness as an individual, that researchers can hope to gain some control over the effect that these can have on any attempt to represent the social world.

This perspective consists in 'objectifying the subject of objectification', that is, deploying 'all the available instruments of objectification (statistical surveys, ethnographic observation, historical research, etc.) in order to bring to light the presuppositions it owes to its inclusion in the object of knowledge'.[9] The assumptions are of three kinds. First, the most accessible are those associated with the subject's position in the public arena, the particular trajectory that led to it, and their social origin and gender. Next come those that constitute the *doxa* specific to each of the different fields of intellectual production (religious, artistic, philosophical, etc.) and, more precisely, those that each individual scholar owes to their position in their own particular field. Finally, and even more profoundly, there are assumptions related to *skholè*, namely leisure, distance from the demands and crises of the world. As a condition underlying the existence of all scholarly fields, *skholè*, along with the 'scholastic vision' that it engenders, is the most complicated to apprehend and manage for those who are immersed in universes where it is taken for granted.[10]

In order to perform reflexivity as Bourdieu conceives it, it is not sufficient to confront these three orders of assumption by making them explicit. For Bourdieu, reflexivity is less an act of attaining conscious awareness, however painstakingly, than an effort to achieve a practical mastery of the social unconscious that inhabits every one of us, along with the effects of the social determinants that weigh on us, invisible effects that the mere will to be lucid is insufficient to detect. Since it is not enough to be aware of the existence of these determinants in the abstract to limit their impact, one way of succeeding is to vary their scope. Awareness can be liberating, as long as we engage with the actual conditions needed for this liberation. A characteristic example of the concrete application of reflexivity for Bourdieu was when he undertook in Béarn the type of investigation that he had carried out in Algeria, enabling him to take into account empirically the effects of distance or proximity generated by the study of a foreign or a familiar society. This procedure determines the way he uses an 'informant' and analyses their nature. In an investigation, informants are always involved in staging themselves and their universe, especially in the presence of a stranger. Far from accepting their point of view as gospel, we must question the social position of the speaker at every turn, and the particular social relationship they entertain with the person questioning them, in order to identify the grains of truth contained in their discourse. This also implies paying attention to the use of technical equipment, such as the tape recorder or the camera, as well as the social composition of the research team[11] – in short, the whole range of the mental or technical faculties that the researcher mobilizes in the survey without realizing that they can help to determine results.

Among the obstacles to scientific knowledge, there is, rather paradoxically, the very fact of holding a scientific viewpoint, characterized by its external position enabling observation over time and at a distance, and defined by its conscious departure from the logic of practice. Thus,

> breaking with the unthinking assumptions of conscious thought, that is, with *scholastic bias*, [leads] the sociologist and economist unable to appropriate their pre-reflexive experience of the world [to insert] scholarly thoughts, driven by the myths of *homo oeconomicus* and the 'theory of rational action', into the behaviour of ordinary economic agents.[12]

Hence the counter-intuitive injunction that Bourdieu enunciates:

> In my opinion, nothing is more false than the universally accepted maxim in the social sciences that the

researcher must not put anything personal into their research. On the contrary, we must constantly refer to our own experience, but not, as is all too often the case, even among the best researchers, in a shame-faced, unconscious, or uncritical manner.[13]

In a late interview, Bourdieu reminds us that reflexivity must be embodied in practical procedures and in their rational use:

I have two important things to teach: (1) strategies for the collective organization of work necessary to gain the autonomy that is the condition of scientific practice; (2) the rational management of intellectual work. Many researchers believe that they must lead their lives as artists, in accordance with a whole mythology. However, the researcher is much more comparable to a top-flight sportsman who must rationalize. Intellectual work has its training regime, which includes managing the team, working as a team, organizing the team, and kitting out the team.[14]

Beyond sociological analysis and practical procedures, reflexivity must still be converted into a disposition incorporated into the scientific *habitus*, that is, exist as 'a *reflexivity reflex*, capable of acting not *ex post*, on the *opus operatum*, but *a priori*, on the *modus operandi*'.[15]

★ ★ ★

Four relatively short and little-known texts by Bourdieu on reflexivity are collected in this volume. They bring to the fore certain largely unnoticed aspects of his practice, which are treated more systematically in *The Logic of Practice* (1980), *Pascalian Meditations* (1997), and *Science of Science and Reflexivity* (2001). The present collection, which forms as it were a review of the question, includes two unpublished texts, an article that was published only in German, and one contributed to the journal *Actes de la recherche en sciences sociales*, but which has never been republished since.

The collection opens with an unpublished work from 1967, 'Epistemology and the Sociology of Sociology'. It was a contribution to a debate held at the Sorbonne on the theme 'What Are the Human Sciences For? (Formalization and Models)'. This debate was organized by the Centre national des jeunes scientifiques (CNJS) and a short-lived journal, *Porisme* (1966–7), which published the work of the CNJS.[16] Other participants were the mathematicians Marc Barbut and André Régnier, the philosopher Jean-Toussaint Desanti, the psychologist Pierre Gréco, and the linguist Nicolas Ruwet. The lecture that Bourdieu gave on this occasion was part of an enquiry into the sociology of science that was taking shape in the CSE and developed initially in two directions: the sociology of scientific vulgarization and the sociology of medicine.[17] The study of the vulgarization of science was conducted in collaboration with the CNJS.[18]

This lecture outlines the programme of a sociology of science characterized by its rejection of an abstract epistemological discourse, in this case discussing the notion of the 'model' which was the official theme of the debate. Bourdieu rejects theoretical and philosophical epistemology and elaborates the argument for making epistemological questions sociological. He adopts a stance that develops reflections made in his studies of Algeria and Béarn, as well as those in progress at the CSE, which amount to a critique of the major epistemological discourses dominant at the time, of which the philosophers of the École normale supérieure, Althusserians, Lacanians, and others, and their *Cahiers pour l'analyse* (1966–9) are a typical example.[19] Like the neopositivist philosophy of science, which was still marginal in France, their work questioned the epistemology, methodology, or logic of science, but in a theoretical mode that ignored scientific practice and its social circumstances, which were at the heart of the programme outlined by Bourdieu. The text that Bourdieu and Passeron wrote around the same time on the relationship between sociology and philosophy in France is a good illustration of the 'sociology of sociology' that Bourdieu calls for in his lecture, seeing it above all as an instrument of epistemological vigilance.[20]

This reflection continues with *The Craft of Sociology* (1968) and *Outline of a Theory of Practice* (1972). According to Bourdieu, Chamboredon, and Passeron, scientific practice must be subjected to an interrogation which, unlike the classic philosophy of knowledge, applies not to 'science made, [. . .] but to science *being made*', that is, not so much to the logic of proof, *ars probandi*, as to that of invention, *ars inveniendi*.[21] In *Outline of a Theory of Practice*, Bourdieu states that 'specialists in epistemological or methodological reflection are condemned to consider the *opus operatum* rather than the *modus operandi*, which implies, in addition to a certain delay, a certain systematic bias'. Shifting the gaze to actual scientific practice expresses the intention to 'disconcert both those who reflect on the social sciences without practising them and those who practise them without reflecting on them'.[22]

The three texts that complete the present volume date from a quarter of a century later and were developed in a historical conjuncture quite different from the rather philosophical-scientific atmosphere that surrounded 'structuralism' in the 1960s. In the meantime, Bourdieu had developed his analysis of scholastic bias and his theory of practice in *Outline of a Theory of Practice* and *The Logic of Practice*. He had also published his seminal article on the scientific field, 'The Specificity of the Scientific Field and the Social Conditions of the Progress of Reason' (1975),[23] which was republished in a slightly revised version the following year in *Actes de la recherche en sciences sociales*, a journal newly created at the CSE and which can be seen as a product of reflexivity in action.

Without mentioning all the stages of his reflection on reflexivity, we can observe that Bourdieu tends to insist more and more on the socio-analytical function of sociology, including the sociology of the sciences: 'any true sociological enterprise is, at one and the same time, a socio-analysis' which allows a certain freedom in relation to determinisms and a 'true re-appropriation of the self'.[24] *Homo Academicus* (1984) undoubtedly played a major part in elaborating this concept as well as applying it to a scholarly universe. For Bourdieu, this work acquired a special status, in the sense that the work of objectification of the academic field went hand in hand with 'a work – a labour in the psychoanalytic sense – upon the subject of objectification. Working on such an object, one is reminded at every moment that the subject of the objectification himself is being objectified.'[25] It is this original process of objectification that did in fact lead to *Science of Science and Reflexivity* as well as to *Sketch for a Self-Analysis* (2004).

In parallel with his questions about science in the making, Bourdieu reflected on the pedagogy of research and the transmission of knowledge and skills, that is, on the research seminar and, from 1982 onwards, on his own lectures at the Collège de France. He returned several times to the difficulties of transmitting the skills of the research profession. At the beginning of his teaching at the Collège de France, he reminded us that the results of his work, all provisional to varying degrees, appeared to him to be 'less important than a certain way of thinking'. What he aims to transmit are not theses or theories, but rather a way of working and a way of thinking, at the heart of which lies the practice of enquiry.

During this same period of the 1970s and 1980s, Robert Merton's philosophy of science and sociology of scientific institutions were to some extent eclipsed by 'science studies', which were becoming increasingly popular. A relativist and 'postmodernist' atmosphere emerged from these studies which, shortly after the publication of the texts by Bourdieu reproduced here, led to the 'Sokal affair' (1996) and the 'science wars'.[26]

In this context, the second text in this volume, 'Narcissistic Reflexivity and Scientific Reflexivity' (1993), which was published only in German, contrasts two conceptions of reflexivity. It emphasizes the fact that reflexivity as Bourdieu sees it is not a narcissistic game in which the scholar looks inward, but rather an effort to engage the procedures of social science in order to objectify scientific work and the social conditions in which it is practised.

The following two texts, although very different from each other in form, pursue this orientation and are linked to the seminar that Bourdieu devoted to the social history of the social sciences for two consecutive years (1995–7) at the École des hautes études en sciences sociales (EHESS). Delivered as an introduction to the second year of the seminar, the text 'Proposal for a Social History of the Social Sciences' (1997) takes up the theme of reflexivity and illustrates it at the same time, as the seminar of these years was organized in an experimental way: the number of people enrolled was much higher than usual, and foreign students in particular were asked to present their reflections on the state of this social history in their country of origin.[27] During this second year, Bourdieu also invited doctoral students, that is, researchers who were less advanced, to present research that was still tentative and provisional. This was not only in order to break with the tradition of the lecture, but also to bring the seminar closer to the situation of research in the making and to try to provide an opportunity for as many people as possible to 'take part in something that resembles a research group'. Aware of the difficulties involved, Bourdieu was convinced that research teaching should be conducted as a search, and that reflexivity helps to fight 'social constraints, whether they are driven by social structures, individual dispositions, or the objectified aspects of the incorporated aspects of the institution'. One of the functions of the seminar is thus to give everyone the freedom to 'look into what you are and what you are doing, in such a way as to open up possibilities that were previously closed'.

Unlike this oral contribution, which was semi-improvised, and distinct from the more elaborate oral format of the lectures at the Collège de France, the final text, 'The Cause of Science: How the Social History of the Social Sciences Can Serve the Progress of These Sciences' (1995), was formatted and written for publication. It functions as an introduction to the two thematic issues of the journal *Actes de la recherche en sciences sociales* devoted to the 'Social History of the Social Sciences'.[28] It can be read first of all as a passionate defence of science in a period of rampant relativism and political reaction, but, more fundamentally, as an explicit formulation of the privileged instrument of reflexivity that the social history of scientific practices provides. While this text elaborates an aspect of the sociological approach proposed by Bourdieu since 1967, it can also be read as a critique of the historicist posture, whose attacks on 'presentism' had become increasingly prevalent. This historicist approach, with its refusal to question the contemporary implications of socio-historical work on science, threatens to undermine reflexivity. Alongside Bourdieu's other texts on the same theme, this volume thus recalls the sometimes misunderstood and, in any case, little practised programme of a reflexive social science.

Jérôme Bourdieu and Johan Heilbron

Editorial Note

To guide the reader, the first names of the authors mentioned have been included on their initial appearance. In some places, the punctuation and typography have been slightly amended to improve the readability of the text. A few corrections necessary for the proper understanding of the text have been made: they are indicated in square brackets. All endnotes have been added by the editors of this volume, except in the last text, published and annotated by Pierre Bourdieu himself, where the additional notes have therefore been indicated as such: '(ed. note)'.

The first text, 'Epistemology and the Sociology of Sociology (1967)', is the transcription of Bourdieu's contribution to a debate, 'What are the Human Sciences for? (Formalization and Models)', which was held in Paris at the Sorbonne in the Descartes amphitheatre on 26 May 1967. Organized jointly by the journal *Porisme*

(1966–7) and the Centre national des jeunes scientifiques (CNJS), this debate brought together Marc Barbut (mathematician), Jean-Toussaint Desanti (philosopher), Pierre Gréco (psychologist), André Régnier (mathematician), and Nicolas Ruwet (linguist). Source of the text: Pierre Bourdieu Archives, file provisionally classified in 'Colloques/Réunions 1965–1967'.

The second text, 'Narcissistic Reflexivity and Scientific Reflexivity (1993)', was published in German under the title 'Narzißtische Reflexivität und wissenschaftliche Reflexivität' (translated into German by Daniel Devoucoux, in Eberhard Berg and Martin Fuchs, eds, *Kultur, soziale Praxis, Text. Die Krise der ethnographischen Repräsentation*, Frankfurt-am-Main, Suhrkamp, 1993, pp. 365–74). The text is dedicated to Loïc Wacquant, Bourdieu's collaborator, professor of sociology at the University of California at Berkeley, and co-author of *An Invitation to Reflexive Sociology* (Cambridge: Polity, 1992). Text source: Pierre Bourdieu Archives, unpublished manuscript.

The third text, 'Proposal for a Social history of the Social Sciences (1997)', is Bourdieu's introduction to the second year of his seminar entitled 'A Social History of the Social Sciences' (1995–7), given at the École des hautes études en sciences sociales (EHESS). Text source: Pierre Bourdieu Archives, unpublished manuscript.

The fourth and final text, 'The Cause of Science: How the Social History of the Social Sciences Can Serve the

Progress of These Sciences (1995)', functioned as an introduction to two thematic issues of the journal *Actes de la recherche en sciences sociales* devoted to the 'Social History of the Social Sciences' (pp. 3–10 of no. 106–7). It takes up some of the themes of a paper presented in 1989 at the Chicago colloquium on 'Social Theory and Emerging Issues in a Changing Society' and published under the title 'Epilogue: On the Possibility of a Field of World Sociology' (in Pierre Bourdieu and James S. Coleman, eds, *Social Theory for a Changing Society*, Boulder, CO: Westview Press/New York: Russell Sage Foundation, 1991, pp. 373–87).

Epistemology and the
Sociology of Sociology
(1967)

Jean-Toussaint Desanti: Thank you very much. It is now time to listen to Bourdieu, to whom I give the floor.

Pierre Bourdieu: I had no intention of talking of models, and since Pierre Gréco[1] has just said more or less what I would have said if I had agreed to discuss them, that has strengthened my resolve.

I would like to try very briefly to raise not the epistemological issue of the model in sociology, but more precisely the sociological question of the conditions in which the problem of models in sociology is posed, in order to try to show that sociology contains within its own bounds the power to reflect on itself, and in particular to reflect on its own scientificity. I do this [. . .] with more than one ulterior motive. I believe that the particular situation of sociology, and more precisely the situation of sociology in relation to the

19

natural sciences and the methods they have to offer, is such that many of the phantasmagorias of a scientific type that some sociologists indulge in are the product of the relationship – experienced as embarrassing or distressing – that sociology and [. . .] the human sciences in general entertain with the natural sciences.

It seems to me that, given the present state of affairs, we cannot reflect on the specific issues raised by the epistemology of the human sciences without reflecting on the social conditions under which these epistemological problems are posed. At the same time, I would like to try to show, or at least indicate, how the scope and repercussions of a certain number of traditional epistemological reflections, elaborated essentially in relation to the natural sciences, can be strengthened, provided that we restore them to their place in a properly sociological context. I shall just remind you of what Gréco said at the beginning, when he described what are more or less the three main positions that sociologists or psychologists adopt, more often implicitly than explicitly, towards the problem of theory; such positions can, as Gaston Bachelard suggested, be grouped into pairs of symmetrical positions in relation to a central epistemological position, whose principal characteristic is to transcend these frequently spurious oppositions.[2] As it stands, sociology is very often [split] into social groups that are organized around epistemological divisions. Which means that the oppositions between formalism and positivism, or between social philosophy and blind hyper-empiricism, which may be described by the epistemologist as pairs of complementary and contradictory positions, are in fact promoted by groups occupying determined positions in an intellectual field, within which they become social positions.

It seems to me, therefore, that it is with reference to the structure of a given epistemological field at a given moment in time that the oppositions take on their real meaning [. . .] (and here we might find the problem of models or, more precisely, the problem of the relationship of sociologists to their models). For example, I think that, in the present [circumstances], it is impossible to understand the epistemological situation of the human sciences without noticing the role that the image of the natural sciences, at once mutilated and mutilating, terri-fying and fascinating, plays in sociologists' own practice. Somebody said earlier, quite rightly, that the practitioners of the human sciences would have more to gain from absorbing the spirit of logical or mathematical procedures than from more external and mechanical techniques. In fact, the relationship between the human sciences and the natural sciences may be described in terms of a logic that is well known in the sociology of contacts between civilizations: because of the dual training mentioned by Marc Barbut, most sociologists have received a literary education and have a perception of the natural sciences defined by the *laws of cultural borrowing*, which means that they perceive the form rather than the function, the external features of the operations rather than the spirit that drives them, so that they mechanically copy the most mechanical aspects of the operations. We could take the example of statistics, which [contains] a whole epistemology: it would be enough to reflect on what it is to make a calculation of error or a test of significance, and so on, to see that the use of the least of these techniques presupposes an extremely acute epistemological awareness, an epistemological awareness which is, as it were, anaesthetized by the logic of borrowing. Ethnologists have often described what they call *nativistic movements*, that is, the kind of 'revivalist' rites whose most famous example is the 'cargo cult'.[3] A number of works by social scientists with scientific pretensions illustrate the cargo cult paradigm admirably.

A fundamental consequence of all this is that when we reflect on the current state of development of the human sciences, when we ask ourselves whether sociology is a science, we are drawing on an extremely simplistic evolutionary schema according to which all the sciences would successively go through the same stages, which leads us to consider sociology as a science in its infancy. This is an absurd proposal, simply because the human sciences will never retrace the steps taken by the other sciences as they are familiar with their itinerary and most of their errors along the way may be due to the fact that they have a false image of the path taken by other sciences.

Sociology has witnessed the emergence of a category of experts in methodological thinking. Through their mediation, the image of the natural sciences, which is both grandiose and terrifying, is in danger of exerting what American psychologists call 'perceptual closure': in presenting as an ideal to be immediately realized an image of science that certain branches of the natural sciences, namely the most formalized, have themselves only tentatively [concretized], there is a risk of producing this effect of premature closure or, on the contrary, of provoking spurious constructions that will have borrowed from the natural sciences only their most caricatural and external features.

That said, can sociology not provide itself with the instruments that would allow it not so much to answer the question of its scientificity, but, more concretely, to help it find its own way to move towards scientificity? If it is true that epistemological positions are linked to the positions occupied in a given intellectual field, I think that the sociology of sociology or, more precisely, the sociology of the social conditions of the production of sociological sciences is one of the fundamental conditions for the progress of sociological knowledge. For example, many epistemological conflicts can be understood in terms of an analysis of the conditions under which sociological researchers are recruited: as long as sociologists do not receive a proper mathematical training sufficient to insulate them from certain fascinations, we will see a sociology of intuition and fantasy continue to flourish alongside a no less fantastical formalism.

It would also be easy to show that a certain type of social organization of intellectual work gives rise to a certain type of epistemology. For example, the bureaucratic division of labour which [divides] scientific staff into those who formulate hypotheses and those who tick boxes or draw graphs goes hand in hand with an epistemological division between formalism and hyper-empiricism.

I think these are facts that sociology can handle, so that we can not only account for a certain type of situation of epistemological conflict, but also see how an analysis of the situation can raise the epistemological awareness of researchers and, by the same token, the relationship they have with all their techniques, and in particular with models.

Sociology could go further, to the point of analysing, for example, the affinity that may exist between an epistemological position [and a social position]: [different views] of the problem of determinism in the human sciences are probably not distributed at random [but] according to the social anchorage and social origins of researchers.

As regards the problem of the model (because I do actually want to talk about it a little), I would simply like to show, by way of example, how a mindset in sociological circles engenders an unfortunate attitude towards all forms of formalization. Methodologists, whose hands are so clean that they have no hands, wallow in their self-satisfied feelings of sinlessness or, better still, of guilt-inducing sinlessness. Our social conditions favour a relationship to models that is quite the opposite of the one described by Gréco, in that they lead sociologists anxious to 'do science' to embrace all the 'chic' methods, from componential analysis to the theory of graphs. However much the instruments of logical control, in particular the model, are, I admit, indispensable aids to epistemological vigilance, they also seem to me to be dangerous in a situation where they very often have the function of anaesthetizing epistemological vigilance.

While I also agree with Gréco in refusing to identify the specific nature of the human sciences as an issue, I believe that we must insist on the specific nature of the relationship that the social sciences entertain with the social conditions under which they are practised. Sociologists must be particularly vigilant in protecting themselves from all surreptitious influence, from all forms of contamination, from the spontaneous sociology that is the outstanding epistemological threat to the human sciences, and in the present state of affairs I see no real defence, other than the sociology of sociology. Not that I think that the sociology of sociology, or the 'socio-analysis' that researchers might practise on themselves, would be enough to protect them once and for all time from all the seductions of the intellectual fashion and 'mood' of the time. I simply think that the conditions for a collective socio-analysis must be established, since each individual researcher undertaking the sociology of their own sociology and of the social conditions capable of inspiring its fundamental assumptions is the victim of an illusion. In order to go beyond a 'self-socio-analysis', which would risk being just another way of attaining a state of sinlessness in order to wallow in the satisfaction of denouncing the guilt of others, it is necessary to [found] a scientific universe in which a generalized interchange of criticism could flourish. And, to use a 'chic' metaphor of the type I have denounced, I would say that the restricted exchange of criticism between accredited opponents – an exchange which, like the restricted exchange of women, is hardly conducive to integration – must be replaced by the interchange of A criticizing B criticizing C criticizing N criticizing A. We would have a scientific community subject to generalized criticism and endowed with institutions in which such criticism is organized (learned societies, journals, etc.), a community absolutely opposed to the all-too-familiar world of ritual polemics between grand theorists.

Thus, in order to make decisive progress, sociology must perhaps seek the weapons needed to arm its progress within its own resources, instead of seeking them at all costs from the more accomplished sciences, which, ultimately, do not offer it the real solutions to its true problems. And as long as the social conditions of scientific practice have not been satisfied, any 'demonstration effect' – to use the vocabulary of ethnologists again – risks leading to productions that do no more than ape a resemblance to the models they claim to imitate. Ultimately, sociology must reclaim its intellectual autonomy because, more than any other science, it is vulnerable to external solicitations – solicitations from those who request surveys which, through financial pressure, for example, can orient research; solicitations born of prevailing ideological demands, whether they be the demands of the dominant groups or of the best-known intellectual groups – the most dangerous of which are not necessarily the usual suspects. This particular vulnerability of sociology requires specifically adapted weapons: this is why we hear people refuse to discuss the problem of models, not because this problematic seems totally devoid of interest, but because, in the current state of scientific debate and sociological science, it could have the function of hiding what I judge to be the real problem. Bachelard said more or less that all discourse on method is a discourse of circumstance.[4] An epistemological discourse, when it comes to sociology, cannot be an omnitemporal discourse: it must refer to a certain social situation in order to prioritize emergencies, without forgetting that, in such social situations, epistemological obstacles have differing strengths, which they do not derive solely from a purely sociological logic. Thus, to illustrate this last proposition simply, we could show that, in the present state of affairs, sociology has to reckon with two major obstacles, at once contradictory and complementary: the danger of formalism to which discussions on the model may lead; and the danger of blind empiricism.

Narcissistic Reflexivity and Scientific Reflexivity

(1993)

For Loïc Wacquant

Until recently, social scientists were hardly inclined to indulge in any real reflection on their practice. And this is especially the case in the dominant traditions, those of English ethnologists (with some famous exceptions, such as Bronisław Malinowski) and American sociologists. This positivist *certitudo sui* is now in peril. Like an organism [with] a defective immune system, the body of Anglo-American scholars seems to be about to succumb to the epidemic of rampant reflexivity that has infected it. This is why, although you can't suspect me of complicity with the scientistic faith, I think it is necessary to recall both what I believe to be the true objective of the search for reflexivity and the properly scientific effects that can be expected from this scientific scrutiny of scientific practice.

* * *

Since I am unable to carry out a systematic examination of all the analyses that claim to be reflexive, I will limit myself to fleshing out the position that I am defending, by briefly situating it in relation to a certain number of the positions that seem to me to be most typical. The self-regarding gaze that the reflexive method requires, in my opinion, goes far beyond the demands of what Wes Sharrock and Bob Anderson call the 'egological point of view'[1] as promoted by ethnomethodology, or reflexivity as Alvin Gouldner conceives it. It is not enough to make the 'lived experience' of the knowing subject explicit; we need to objectify the social conditions that render this experience, and, more precisely, this act of objectification, possible. For Gouldner, objectivity remains a project, albeit a vague one, which has never been truly implemented. What we need to objectify is not *only* the researcher in terms of their unique biography, nor the intellectual *Zeitgeist* that inspires their work (which is Gouldner's approach in his analysis of Talcott Parsons[2]), but the position they occupy within the academic space, and the 'biases' written into the organizational structure of the discipline, that is to say, into the whole collective history of the specialism at issue: I am thinking in particular of the unconscious *assumptions* that are embodied in the theories, problematics, and ([especially] the national) categories of scholarly understanding. Which leads us to make the scientific field itself both the *subject* and the *object* of our reflexive analysis.

Having said that, I hardly need to state that I have little sympathy for what Clifford Geertz calls the 'diary disease',[3] that explosion of narcissism which has followed long years of positivist repression: true reflexivity is not about indulging in *post festum* reflections on fieldwork; it has little in common with 'textual reflexivity', nor with falsely sophisticated analyses of the 'hermeneutic process of cultural interpretation' and the construction of reality through ethnographic recording. I believe that its intentions are in fact profoundly opposed to the act of observing an observer, which in George Marcus and Michael Fischer or Renato Rosaldo,[4] or even Clifford Geertz, tends to fall victim to the sway of the charms of self-observation, which is ultimately easier and more gratifying than confronting the uncomfortable realities of the 'field'. When it becomes an *end in itself*, instead of being directed towards refining and strengthening the instruments of knowledge, this falsely radical denunciation of ethnographic writing as 'poetic and political', in the words of James Clifford and George Marcus,[5] necessarily leads to 'interpretive scepticism', according to Steve Woolgar,[6] or even to nihilism (as do the various forms of the so-called 'strong' programme in the sociology of science).

As for ethnomethodology, I approve all the more sincerely of the project it has adopted, to make explicit the *folk theories* that social agents [act out] in their practice, since I myself – partly from the same sources (Edmund Husserl and Alfred Schütz in particular, and also the tradition of cognitive anthropology committed to analysing primitive forms of classification), partly from the reflections of epistemologists such as Gaston Bachelard and Georges Canguilhem, who were committed to flushing out the assumptions underlying common knowledge – had simultaneously come to devise a programme of analysis of the 'prenotions' (in Émile Durkheim's sense[7]) that social agents deploy in their construction of social reality. But, as we showed in *The Craft of Sociology*,[8] science cannot make the objectification of the forms and contents of common knowledge its exclusive and ultimate object. Such an analysis can be no more than one of the moments of research, a particularly powerful instrument for *breaking* with the illusions of common sense and, in this way, a prerequisite for the scientific construction of the object.

Moreover, although it is fashionable to recall that, as Husserl and Schütz have shown, the primary experience of the social is a relationship of immediate belief that leads us to accept the world as self-evident, we must look behind description to try to discover the conditions of possibility of this doxic experience. We can see that the coincidence between objective and embodied structures, which creates the illusion of immediate understanding, is a special case in the universe of possible relations to the world, the case of indigenous experience. The great virtue of the experience of the foreign world as encountered by ethnologists is that it immediately reveals that these conditions are not universally satisfied, as phenomenology would have us believe when it (unwittingly) universalizes a reflection based on the special case of the phenomenologist's given relationship to their own society.

It is therefore necessary to sociologize the phenomenological analysis of *doxa* as an unquestioned submission to the everyday world, not only in order to establish that it is not universally valid for every perceiving and acting subject, but also to discover that, when it is practised in certain social situations, especially among the dominated, it represents the most radical form of acceptance of the world as it is, the most absolute form of conformism. No embrace of the established order is more wholly comprehensive than this infra-political relation of doxic self-evidence, which leads people to accept as natural certain conditions of existence that someone socialized under different conditions would find revolting, since they would not perceive them through categories of perception derived from that same world.

The political implications of the *doxa* are never more clearly seen than in the symbolic violence that is exerted on the dominated and, in particular, on women. I am thinking in particular of the kind of socially contrived agoraphobia that leads women to exclude themselves from public activities and ceremonies from which they are in fact excluded (according to the dichotomy setting the public and masculine against the private and feminine), [especially] in the realm of official politics. Or the fact that they think that if they are able to cope with these situations, they are bound to pay for it with extremes of stress that match the intensity of the effort required to overcome the acceptance of exclusion that is inscribed deep within their bodies. Thus, a narrowly phenomenological or ethnomethodological analysis leads us to overlook the historical foundations and, by the same token, the political significance of this relationship of an automatic correlation between subjective and objective structures.

The form of reflexivity that seems to me to be the most scientifically fruitful is entirely paradoxical, since it is profoundly *anti-narcissistic*. This is undoubtedly one of the reasons why it is so little practised and why its results provoke so much resistance. The properties that this sociology of sociology discovers, which are completely opposed to an intimate and self-indulgent return to the private *person* of the sociologist, are neither singular nor extraordinary; they are common, for the most part, to entire categories of researchers (and therefore banal and not very 'exciting' for the naïvely curious). [This sociology] questions the charismatic image that intellectuals tend to have of themselves, and also their propensity to think that they are free from all social determinations. It reveals the social at the heart of the individual, the impersonal hidden behind the intimate.

* * *

Having thus briefly characterized reflexivity as I conceive it in relation to other forms of analysis that boast the same intentions, I can now outline the three major phases of this reflexive analysis or, amounting to the same thing, the three forms of 'bias' that it leads us to discover and invites us to overcome. First, it is a question of objectifying – as has often been done both in the strict and in the wider Marxist traditions, from Georg Lukács to Karl Mannheim – the *social conditions of production of the producer*, that is, the properties, especially the techniques and the interests, which they owe to their social, sexual, or ethnic origins. But as I have shown in my work on the sociology of literature [for example] (although the same would apply to the sociology of science or law), you can leave it at that and still miss the point: for example, one of the intentions of *Homo Academicus*[9] is to show that when we map cultural products directly onto the economic, social, or political conditions that have allegedly produced the producers, or the social classes for whom they are supposed to produce, we are guilty of what I call a 'short-circuit paralogism', by establishing a direct link between very distant terms, and omitting the essential mediatory force, which is the relatively autonomous social universe constituted by the field of cultural production.

We must therefore also take as our object this microcosm, this autonomous social world, within which

34

agents struggle for stakes of a very specific nature and obey interests which may be [perfectly] disinterested in other respects, from a financial point of view, for example. It is therefore necessary to shed light on the position that the analyst occupies, no longer in the social structure in the broad sense, but in the scientific (or academic) field, that is, in the objective space of the social positions available at a given moment in a given scientific universe (as indicated, roughly speaking, in a sentence such as 'Mr X is an *Assistant Professor* of Sociology at Columbia').

However, to stop here would be to miss the point, that is, the set of (unconscious) assumptions whose very principle lies neither in the social position nor in the specific position of the sociologist within the field of cultural production (nor, by the same token, within a space of possible theoretical and methodological positions), but in the invisible determinations that are inscribed at the heart of the scholar's position. As soon as we observe the social world, our perception of this world is affected by a 'bias' linked to the fact that, in order to study, describe, and talk about it, we have to withdraw from it more or less completely. The *theorist or intellectualist bias* consists in forgetting to factor into the theory of the social world which we construct the fact that it is the product of a theoretical gaze, of a 'contemplative eye' (*theôrein*) that tends to apprehend the world as a *spectacle*, as a (theatrical and mental) representation, as a set of signs needing to be interpreted, rather than a set of concrete problems calling for practical solutions. A truly reflexive sociology must be constantly on its guard against this 'epistemocentrism', this 'scholarly ethno-centrism', which implies ignoring everything that marks the specific difference between theory and practice, and projects onto the description and analysis of a practice the representation that the analyst may have of the object, observing it from outside, from a distance and from on high.

Just as the anthropologist who constructs a genealogy has a relation to 'kinship' that has nothing in common with that of a Kabyle father who has to solve a practical and urgent problem such as finding a suitable husband for his daughter, so the sociologist who studies the school system makes 'use' of the school in a way that has nothing in common with that of a father looking for a good school for his son. [In other words], so long as they do not submit to analysis their own status as a *scholar* whose social condition includes the possibility of *skholè* (that is to say, leisure, distance from necessity, urgency, and immediate need, in short, from practice, which are the conditions required to provide the objec-tifying distance and withdrawal that define the scientific gaze), the researcher is exposed to what I call, after John Austin, the *scholastic bias*.[10] In failing to analyse the implications of the act of thinking the world, in failing to withdraw from the world and from action in the world in order to think it, the thinker is liable to substitute, unthinkingly, *their own mode of thinking* for that of the agents they are analysing, who lack the leisure (and, very often, the desire) to analyse themselves. [The thinker is also liable] to invest their object with the fundamental assumptions that are lodged in the fact of *thinking* it *as an object*, instead of having *to deal with it as an object*, to handle it and make it their business (*prâgma*). Moreover, they run the risk of imbuing their acts of knowledge with all the instruments of unthought thought resulting from the long labours of thinking accomplished by their predecessors, such as genealogy or the questionnaire.

But you may ask: are these analyses not the product of a purely epistemological point of honour, devoid of any practical consequences? In fact, we should recall here the whole series of scientific effects produced by this reflection, which is not its own end in itself. And show, for example, how reflecting on rules and the meaning of behaviour designed to 'obey a rule' (as outlined by Ludwig Wittgenstein[11]) leads us to fundamentally rethink the theory of kinship and to substitute a logic of strategy (generated, without any express intention, by the *habitus*) for the logic of the rule. Thus, far from leading to scepticism or nihilism, the sociology of sociology encourages a more rigorous exercise of the scientific method. The fact that scientific knowledge owes many of its most fundamental properties to the conditions of its production (the *skholè* and all its implications) not being those of practice does not lead to a denial of the validity of theoretical knowledge. On the contrary, a clear knowledge of the *limits of theoretical knowledge* makes it possible to avoid the 'scholastic fallacy', which consists in projecting into analysis all the errors of *epistemocentrism*, that is, the tendency of scholars to picture the agents they study in their own image: I could cite, in any order, the various forms (whether right- or left-wing) of 'rational action theory', Chomsky's vision of linguistic competence and its usage, Lévi-Straussian structuralism, and so on.[12]

* * *

Thus, contrary to what the ordinary representation of self-knowledge as an exploration of personal depths suggests, the most intimate truth of our true nature – the most unthinkable unthought – is also inscribed in objectivity, and in particular in the history of the social positions we have held in the past and occupy in the present. Paradoxically, it is through the objectification of the most objective social conditions of thought that we can most surely access the most specific characteristics of the thinker's subjectivity. Social history and the sociology of sociology, understood as an exploration of sociologists' scientific unconscious in making explicit the genesis of the problems, categories of thought, and instruments of analysis that they draw on, constitute an absolute prerequisite to scientific practice. Sociologists can only give themselves some chance of escaping the social conditions of which they, like everyone else, are the product, on condition that they turn against themselves the weapons furnished by their science; on condition that they arm themselves with the knowledge of the social determinations liable to constrain them and, more especially, with the scientific analysis of all the constraints and limitations linked to a position and a trajectory determined within a field, in an attempt to neutralize the effects of these determinations.

Far from ruining the foundations of social science, the sociology of the social determinants of sociological practice is the only conceivable basis for a possible freedom from these determinations. And it is only on condition that sociologists claim the full use of this freedom, by systematically submitting to this analysis, that they can produce a rigorous science of the social world which, far from imprisoning the agents within the straitjacket of a rigid determinism, offers them the wherewithal of a profoundly liberating awareness. This critical analysis of the social determinants of scientific work can only be fully effective if it is not the responsibility of each researcher, relying on the sole force of their lone vigilance, but of all the occupants of the rival scientific positions that compose the scientific field. In order to find fulfilment, reflexivity must be institutionalized, on the one hand, in the mechanisms of the field, in particular in the social logic of scientific discussion and evaluation, and, on the other hand, in the dispositions of the agents.

Adopting the viewpoint of reflexivity does not mean renouncing objectivity; it means making the effort to account for the empirical 'subject' in the same terms used for the objectivity constructed by the scientific subject (in particular by situating it in a given place in social space-time) and, in so doing, gaining awareness and (potential) mastery of the constraints that can affect the scientific subject through all its attachments to the empirical subject, with its interests, impulses, and assumptions – attachments that it must loosen in order to fully constitute itself as a scientific subject. We should also search the scientifically constructed object to discover the social conditions creating the potential of the 'subject' (for example, the *skholè* and the whole inherited tradition of problems, concepts, and methods that makes its activity possible) and the possible limits of its acts of objectification. This will force us to repudiate the absolutist claims of classical objectivity, but without thereby leading to relativism: given that, as we have seen, the subject and the object of reflexive analysis are ultimately nothing other than the scientific field itself, and the conditions of possibility of the scientific 'subject' and those of its object are one and the same, any progress in the knowledge of the social conditions of production of the scientific 'subject' corresponds to a progress in the knowledge of the scientific object, and vice versa. This is never more clearly seen than when research takes as its object the scientific field itself, which is the true subject of scientific knowledge.

Proposal for a Social History
of the Social Sciences
(1997)

Today I would like to briefly explain the topic on the poster: 'A Social History of the Social Sciences'. But first I would like to tell you how I hope to work with you. Last year's seminar [1995–6], for those who followed it, was a rather special case. All the seminars that I've led here have been special cases, because I keep changing the formula, for the simple reason that the conditions in which we hold a seminar are such that it is very difficult to be satisfied with the result. In order to hold a genuine research seminar, you really need a small audience of no more than fifteen or twenty people. This is a threshold beyond which it is very difficult to work. This limitation and the selection it implies have many disadvantages. If we were to open up completely, we would have an audience of the type I usually have at the Collège de France, which is more like a *public meeting* than a working group. The solution I have adopted here is a compromise between the two, [in other words] a selective opening.

Last year, therefore, in practising this measure of openness, I gave the floor to a series of researchers, all already at a very advanced stage in their work, most of whom were university professors, had published books, and were used to dealing with large audiences and giving presentations to large groups. Of course, the disadvantage of this formula is that it reinforces the formal academic distance between the master and the researchers. It is not very conducive to the kind of real discussion that could take place in a seminar of about fifteen people. This year, I shall try [therefore] to give the floor alternately to people who are relatively more junior, who are in the second or third year of their thesis, and then to others who are much more advanced, like those of last year. I will try to ensure that, for example, there are several successive presentations of a theme, so that you see less advanced people presenting research in a less advanced state. I think this is important: in France we are not familiar with the seminar genre. We have been raised in the Catholic tradition of the sermon and the *ex cathedra* lecture, and for largely historical reasons, the French tradition does not easily welcome the genuine seminar, which is something very difficult and very demanding. What we call a seminar in France is often a disorganized lecture. It has all the disadvantages of a lecture and all the disadvantages of 'laissez-faire'. In order to cater for the contradiction I mentioned at the beginning, that is, to try to give as many people as possible the opportunity to take part in something that resembles a research group, without lapsing into the *ex cathedra* lecture, I would like to try to make these seminars more hybrid and ambivalent. But academic traditions are very difficult to change. They form a structured space, they are an assembly of social definitions, and they are also a *habitus*: people are going to bring their own particular *habitus*, and they are going to invest the objectified institution with their own incorporated institution, which may – or may not – match the official definition of the objectified institution.

I am aware of the extreme difficulty of what I am trying to do. There are too many of us for even the people most eager to participate and discuss to do so. In addition, there are perhaps my own dispositions, which are also the product of historical conditions. All this means that what I would like to do this year will function at 50 per cent, with a great deal of wasted energy on both sides and a [considerable] proportion of disappointment. That said, I don't think it means you have to give up. One of the ways we can fight these social constraints, whether they are driven by social structures, individual dispositions, or the objectified aspects of the incorporated aspects of the institution, is precisely by objectifying these constraints, the awareness of which provides a measure of freedom, which is why I am indulging in this preamble.

One of the functions of this seminar should be to discover possible research topics. I think this is a problem that faces young researchers. The choice of a research topic is one of the objects of reflexive sociology, of a social history of social sciences: how do people choose their research? Are we chosen by our research or do we choose our research? What does it mean to choose? What is the nature of this encounter between a disposition and a research proposal? Are we really the subjects of our research? I think that one of the functions of this whole seminar on the social history of the social sciences is to give everyone, whoever you may be, the freedom to look into what you are and what you are doing, in such a way as to open up possibilities that were previously closed.

My dearest ambition for this enterprise would be to transform the seminar into a kind of large study group. For I think that research teaching is a process of searching. And the reason why teaching through public lectures is so disappointing is that you learn about everything but you learn how to do nothing. You can hear a magnificent exegesis of Max Weber without being able to mount a single operation in the way that Weber would have done, and without assimilating any Weberian reflexes. Now, one of the aims of teaching research is not to produce *lectores*, people who rabbit on about texts – France is already full of them – but to produce *auctores*, people who are capable of appropriating methods, theories, and readings, in order to do something with them.

I think research is something very difficult, which you don't get into just by learning *topoi*. Perhaps it also involves a kind of conversion. In the small-scale seminar, the conversion was gradual and, from Easter onwards in general (every year I regretted the time we had lost), the group started to function as a group. People met up, worked together, and helped each other with their theses, and so on. Can we do the equivalent here? I'm not sure. What I can say is that this would be my ideal definition. A framework within which everyone here would at some point, perhaps this year, perhaps next year, or even later, make a contribution to this enterprise called 'a social history of the social sciences'. It could be an interview with a researcher at the CNRS [Centre national de la recherche scientifique], there are thousands of subjects. . . Everyone would decide to make a small contribution, asking a question or telling their tale – 'How did I choose my subject?'. . . All of which means that you can take the floor, not only to ask a question, but also to say: 'What you are saying makes me think of . . .' For example, in the successful small-group seminars, there was a wonderful moment when, on hearing a specialist in Brazilian folk medicine talk about her object of study, a researcher busy studying musicians in provincial conservatories would say: 'That makes me think of . . .' This is the real seminar effect. So I hope that you can, in one way or another, starting today if possible, perhaps later, participate actively in several ways, by asking for clarification or putting wider-ranging questions that you have encountered in connection with your research (possibly, for those who are too shy, you can pass me a small piece of paper with your surname, first name, and a question, and I will try to answer it, either next time or on the spot).

* * *

I hope that this rather long preamble has not been superfluous. Why a 'social history of the social sciences'? I don't want to present a full justification. Everything that I could say would be a development of the idea of reflexivity that I have been promoting for a long time, and I think that at least some of you have read, in *An Invitation to Reflexive Sociology*,[1] for example, a whole section devoted to this problem.

First of all, briefly, as I said last year, 'reflexivity' is not to be understood in the traditional sense of the philosophical *doxa*: reflexivity is not reflection in the sense of *cogitatio cogitationis*, that is, thinking about thinking, reflecting in my thought on my thoughts. It is not a simple return of the knowing subject towards itself, the knowing subject trying to know itself. Reflexivity as I understand it is indeed that, but it passes through a process of objectification. The knowing subject, in the case of a sociologist, a historian, an ethnologist, or even an economist, is someone who possesses techniques of knowledge that they can apply to themselves, the knowing subjects, and more precisely to the social universe in which such a knowing subject is inserted. This social universe can be understood on two levels: as the social space as a whole and also as the position of the researcher, of the discipline, or of a particular sector of the discipline in the overall social space.

Then we can apply this process of objectification to what I call the 'field' of the social sciences, and objectify this space in order to find a number of properties hidden from the knowing subject itself. This is why it is very different from a classic reflexivity. The hypothesis is that the knowing subject does not have access by simple reflection to the essence of its own nature, of its own activity. In order to have access to these, a researcher must make a detour through the objective conditions which produced them in their present state and which frame their actions. In other words, it is a question of practising sociology as we always do, but on the universe of the social sciences, on our own world, our own field.

The reason I chose this topic is because, for the participants, this kind of object can bring two kinds of benefit.[2] It can [provide] the benefits of a seminar on any subject (homosexuality, art history, Quattrocento painting, anything), that is to say, concepts, methods, ways of working. A seminar is not just a place where you hear someone talk about their research. We want to see how a researcher does their research. It is very difficult, because very few people know how to do it, it is an art. The word 'art', as Émile Durkheim somewhere says, designates a practical way of doing things which does

47

not necessarily imply self-knowledge. There is nothing mysterious about the arts. All the fine phrases churned out about creators and their unfathomable creations are just as true for a carpenter or a grocer, for people like us. The art of walking can be learned: there are schools where young girls from the working classes who want to become models are taught to walk (where we see that walking is an art, but that there are some who have acquired it without knowing it and others who have to pay to learn it). That said, when an art is truly acquired, the person who practises it best is the one who explains it worst. This is true of research teaching. If so many people think that teaching research is easy, it is because they do not know what research is. They have no trouble communicating because they have nothing at all to communicate, but even those who do have something to communicate can have a lot of trouble doing it, and I know a lot of very good researchers who would be hard pressed to tell you how to read a statistical table well, or how to make a good ethnographic description. Most of what needs to be communicated is implicit, practical, and for a seminar like this, the closest analogy would be a Quattrocento studio where there are pupils at work and then the master painter comes up behind them and says, 'I wouldn't do it like that.' That would be the ideal. The master is to be taken in a much less pompous sense than in the French academic version: the master here resembles a master of arms, a judo instructor, a master of the martial arts, a trainer; a good research director has more in common with a rugby coach than with a Sorbonne professor. A rugby coach is not necessarily capable of articulating the formal theory of practice or the theory of how to transmit it. There is nothing more difficult than interviewing someone about a practical skill. It is the sociological version of 'art for art's sake'.

We all have an art of living, and the *habitus* is an art of living. The art of living is something that does not involve explicit self-knowledge. The problem of making something explicit is particularly acute for people whose profession is not to explicate. The further we move away from what I call scholastic universes, from the universes of *skholè* in the sense of 'leisure', the more people find it difficult to express their art of living, to say what they do, how they do it, and so on. This is what was terribly misunderstood about *The Weight of the World*:[3] it was a rather desperate attempt to raise to the level of discourse something that can only be explained with great difficulty in any case, even by a painter. Until the nineteenth century, people used to say 'dumb as a painter' (it was often writers who said that) – Marcel Duchamp was the first to rebel. In general, painters, with the exception of Eugène Delacroix, who was the first to pass his baccalaureate, were not very well educated.[4] They had a formidable mastery of what they were doing, but they didn't know how to say anything about it, or at least when they spoke about it, it sounded very stupid, especially to people officially certified as intelligent. These painters and suchlike didn't have an intellectual grasp of their knowledge, and this is very generally true, *a fortiori*, lower down the social hierarchy, that is to say, as we move away from the worlds where people have the time to learn the techniques of exegesis, and learn the mastery of language. [. . .] All the Heidegger–Hölderlin literature on the silences of the peasant,[5] Martin Heidegger by the fireside with his peasant, and so forth, is a literary notation of the fact that language skills are unequally distributed, and that this unequal distribution is never more obvious than when it comes to expressing something that is especially difficult to express, which is what I am, what I do, and how I do it.

The problem of explicating the arts, seen as ways of being and ways of doing, is one of the most central problems of sociology, which many sociologists never encounter. They draft questionnaires . . . It is also a problem for ethnologists. There is an ethnologist who was very important for me in my youth, Bronisław Malinowski. He is the only person, I think, who has developed at length the idea that the most important thing about practices is the manner in which they are performed.[6] Indeed, for an ethnologist, one of the almost insurmountable difficulties is that, in order to detect differences between manners of doing things, you have to be very well acquainted with the different manners; and manners, as we know, are subtle, elusive, and indescribable. They are always extremely difficult to pin down, they are something intangible and, when we do grasp them, we don't know how to express them.

[It's as if] I were to ask you to make a subtle description of something seen in a television programme, like a sour smile, a superior smile, or a forced smile. (Fortunately, by the way, we have ordinary language, which is based on thousands of years of observation, to help with the practical description of manners of doing things.)

I hadn't planned to tell you this at all. It occurred to me in connection with art and, I think, with the logic of reflexivity. Last year, I said very briefly that one of the aims of reflexivity was to make explicit three levels of implicitness, linked to three levels of implication which concern us all. First level: we are implicated in the social space overall and there is an implicit dimension to our overall social involvement, to our position in the overall social space at any one moment, and over time; we have both a position and a trajectory. Second level: we are a position in the field, in the space of our actions, in the sociological or religious field, for instance. One of the objectives of this social history of the social sciences that I want you to undertake is to obtain information on the structure of the field of social sciences in France since 1945, perhaps in a global context. One of the problems is to know whether we can limit our research to the French field, whether in order to understand what is happening in the French field we might not need to know [its position] in the global field of social sciences. [. . .] As we locate our position in the field, so we shall discover at the same time what is implicit. Whenever we discover an implication, we discover the implicit.

Third level of implication: membership of what I call the scholastic universes – the etymological origin is the Greek word *skholè*, which is the root of 'scholastic' and of 'school', and means 'leisure'. Insofar as we have all attended school, often a very long time ago, and still are at school, either as a teacher or as a researcher, we still inhabit the scholastic universe, and what lies deepest in our unconscious is everything connected with membership of this universe. Because we take to it like ducks to water, because belonging to the scholastic universe is associated with our most deep-seated unconscious dispositions.

I have distinguished three levels that range from the most superficial to the most profound. First level: insertion in the social field; you'd have to be very naïve, especially in the light of the traditional Marxist critiques of class or gender, not to wonder about the relationship between what someone says and their social position. The danger of these things remaining implicit and unconscious is relatively small. Second level: the field; this is already almost totally unconscious because the field is not formulated as such and people, whether they are transmitters or receivers, are not aware that what they say can be linked in one way or another to holding a position in a field, itself situated in a position in a space. Third level: the repercussions of membership of the scholastic universes; belonging to scholastic universes is associated with an implicit, scholastic disposition that the English philosopher John Austin refers to as the *scholastic view* or *doctrine*.[7] He does not go into detail, but in fact, whatever we do or write, whether we record a document or conduct an interview, for instance, we are always viewing it through our scholastic lens, and in my opinion, one of the main aims of reflexivity is to try to counter the effects of this scholastic purview.

If there is one thing that the scholastics misunderstand, it is the arts, because their own art is unconscious to them; they have incorporated it like everyone else, they have incorporated the categories of thought and the patterns of perception; and this set of incorporated dispositions is the source of their perception of others. These incorporated dispositions are dispositions that we [integrate] when we are in a position to study the world without being engaged in it. This was one of my first experiences. I was working on an article, 'Bachelorhood and the Peasant Condition',[8] published in the 1960s, about a village I knew very well, having spent my entire childhood and adolescence there; I had deliberately taken this object as a kind of epistemological experiment. (It's the same thing for *Homo Academicus*,[9] it's a bifocal object.) I was hoping, on the one hand, to find why some people are single and others are not, why they don't get a girl, why the girls move away, and[, on the other hand,] to question [my] questioning and understand the difference between my attitude and the kind of explanation I could give, as opposed to the explanations given me by the people I had played bowls with, people who were my *alter egos*. What is entailed in having the privilege of withdrawing from the world in order to think it? If the person in the process of withdrawing from the world in order to reflect on it doesn't reflect on the effect on their thinking of their withdrawal in order to reflect on it, they reflect badly. Their thoughts on the people who do not enjoy conditions where you can withdraw from the world in order to think it are inadequate: these people inhabit the world of practice and, being in that world, provide answers with their practice to questions that have been articulated from a scholastic standpoint. We therefore need to investigate the possibility of a theoretical view of the non-theoretical, and raise the question of the difference between theoretical theory and practice.

These questions are obviously present behind the research topic that I am offering this year. It is a matter of questioning not only the social universe within which the social sciences are practised, but also the scholastic properties of this universe, which can affect the professional practices of the people who are lodged in it. For example, to return to *The Weight of the World*, this was a book that was read by scholastic professionals who said to themselves: 'But what are they doing? How can they ask such questions?', and so on, without seeing that the main intention of the questioning was to question the questioning, and in particular the mismatch between the questioner and the respondent in terms of the scholastic relationship to the world. Plato says: 'To form an opinion is to speak.'[10] This means that our opinion has an implicit dimension – an implicit dimension that is the last thing we professionals of *logos*, of discourse, are likely to notice. An opinion is a discourse, and to opine, to state an opinion, is to raise something to the level of discourse instead of muttering 'oh, oh' or 'ah, ah' or nothing at all. This calculated 'opining', which entails articulating something explicitly in discourse, is not self-evident. It is only self-evident in scholastic worlds where we are professionals of opinion and even experts in personal opinion. I refer you to an old article from the 1970s called 'Questions de politique'[11] in *Actes de la recherche en sciences sociales*, where there is a long *topos* on the cult of personal opinion.

For us, it goes without saying that opining is talking, that one can state opinions and, secondly, that we inhabit worlds where personal opinion – which is one step further – is explicitly valued and encouraged. We constantly make marginal comments like 'banal, personal, trivial, common', and so on. There is a sort of premium on personal opinion. And if we take the case of writing, we could assemble a whole string of quotes, from writers of every persuasion, saying: 'To exist is to be personal,' that is, individual. But this implicit attitude is tacitly pursued by the humblest IFOP [French Institute of Public Opinion] pollster. From parenthesis to parenthesis, I have digressed, but there is nonetheless a common thread. The case of the survey situation is typical of the reflexivity that I am advocating because, in order to arrive at a true reflection of what

I do when I interview someone, I have to go through a prolonged process of objectification. First of all, I have to objectify my social position, the social gap between me and the interviewee. It's obvious enough, but many sociologists forget it: the social gap between a professor at the Collège de France and a young Arab lad who has just been dismissed from his CAP [vocational competence certificate/apprenticeship] is as plain as the nose on your face. We then have to objectify the position in the field. Where does this lead? I can, for example, ask questions that make me look smarter than a rival. They ask questions of opinion, I ask questions of fact. If you start to use your reflexive eyes, you can see an incredible number of scientific acts which we believe to be free and autonomous but which are [in reality] determined by relationships of rivalry within the field, by effects of position within the field, and so on. We need to proceed with the objectification of this space, which is that of the cultural producers, who are the product of quite specific social conditions: scholastic conditions of withdrawal from temporal pressure, of leisure. We could show, for example, how the economist Gary Becker, with his theory of 'human capital'[12] – which is an example that occurs to me at random –, did not think for a second that the production of human capital was subject to social conditions. But in order to understand any cultural production whatsoever, we have to take into account the fact that the person producing it is the product of circumstantial social conditions of production (being outside the world, withdrawing from the world in order to think about it) as well as diachronic, historical ones, such as having attended school and then enjoyed the *skholè* since early childhood. This is how we can reinterpret the statistics on school success. If you see that in order to spend a long time in school, you have to be born into the scholastic universe, you see that you cannot dismiss the *skholè* by saying: 'It's one variable among others.'

Scholastic bias will be all the more powerful the more unconscious its victim – and the more distant, in this respect, from those with whom they are going to communicate. If they are an ethnologist, they work with people who are in societies where survival is a permanent emergency, or if they work on social strata of their own society that are far removed from the scholastic universe, this social and cultural gap can become a kind of total barrier to understanding. I think that in these cases reflexivity is a *sine qua non* for understanding. A huge part of what is written in the social sciences is the product of scholastic bias, that is to say, of people who, unaware of their scholastic bias, put scholastic heads onto non-scholastic bodies. That's what I mean by reflexivity, that's how this social history of the social sciences can be useful for ordinary everyday practice, whether you're interviewing a journalist or a cleaning lady. . .

I thought that this subject could be important because it is doubly profitable: it allows you to reap the benefits that you would gain from any seminar and the benefits of reflexivity, insofar as the methods, theories, techniques, and concepts of the case are applied to your own world, that is to say, to yourself. You can learn what you might learn in a seminar by hearing a specialist talk about folk medicine in Brazil: how she studies it, how she constructs her object, and the like. You will have the usual issues dealt with by sociology, but, in addition, you will reap the benefit of the reflexivity which, in my opinion, is perhaps the most important thing. To illustrate my point, I could refer you to *Homo Academicus*.[13] Even more than the work on celibacy that I told you about,[14] *Homo Academicus* is a typical reflexive undertaking. It is research that has an apparent object, which is the French university in the years before 1968, the structure of this field, the hierarchy of faculties, the position of the arts faculty, and so on. But there is also another object, that is, those who normally take other social agents as their object: geographers, historians, and economists, and so on, are people who are socially mandated to speak with authority about the social and economic world. To take the faculties, the conflict of the faculties, in the words of Immanuel Kant, as an object is to take as objects subjects who have a legitimate knowledge of their object; obviously, the author of the book himself, who is part of the object and cannot forget it for one minute.

In passing, I said rather hastily earlier that we are all scholastic. I think that many acts of research which for a long time I instinctively perceived as errors (I remember a questionnaire in which a French sociologist who always talks about empirical investigation and who has never done any investigation asked: 'How many social classes do you think there are?') were driven by this *scholastic bias*. More generally, I think that as scholastics, whatever our political or religious stance, we are liable to speak the same scholastic language. I could give examples of errors shared by Heideggerians and Marxists. I refer you to issue 5 of *Actes de la recherche en sciences sociales*,[15] a big issue where I juxtaposed a kind of ironic analysis of the rhetoric of Louis Althusser and Étienne Balibar and an analysis of the rhetoric of Martin Heidegger. Although I didn't say so at the time, I was attacking the sacred cows of the scholastic unconscious, and if in addition I had said that what interested me was everything that these sacred cows had in common, even though they appeared to be totally opposed in the political space, I would have been considered subnormal. Twenty years on, you can admit it. Every day, I see examples of deep agreement between people who seemingly agree on nothing.

Where sociologists are concerned, the scholastic bias is particularly catastrophic. A sociologist whose job is partly to understand and make explicit the practice, and perhaps the discourse, of people who are in a non-scholastic situation, who have not been the product of the social conditions of production which are needed in order to understand scholastic problems and answer scholastic questions, and so on, is bound to make mistakes. One of the errors is juridicism, which was one of the first clues to discovering the scholastic bias. When I was working as an ethnologist on the Béarn peasants, I was confronted with studies that were juridical. Around the 1900s, jurists were drawing on varying degrees of juridicism in their studies. There were works that started out from the law and investigated the practices. Some of the ethnological studies took a number of theories, such as the theory of kinship, from Roman law. This was the crudest form of juridicism. I had come across a more subtle form of juridicism with jurists who, in the 1900s, started out not from laws – in this case there were none, it was Béarn, a region ruled by custom – but from notarial acts, in order to reconstitute matrimonial strategies and the logic of matrimonial exchanges. For example, in the books devoted to matrimonial customs in the countries of the *langue d'oc*, there were inevitably long chapters on what was called the *tournadot*, the restitution of the dowry. In fact, in the population I studied, there was not a single divorce. So the restitution of the dowry was an absolutely pointless clause, but it was of capital importance in the writings. Juridicism, as a tendency to deduce practices from the rule which supposedly produces them, is a constant temptation for ethnology, which can be reinforced by the capital available to the ethnologist. In the case of North Africa, many amateur ethnologists were civil servants who had a juridical training and whose thinking drew on the cultural instruments at their disposal (this is also true of Black Africa). But juridicism is a spontaneous philosophy of action that is inherent in the scholastic vision. It is the spontaneous philosophy of action that you find in Claude Lévi-Strauss with the theories of the rule,[16] of preferential marriage as determined by rules. All the social uses of the rule made by ethnologists are based on a philosophy of action whose model is the legal model of applying a rule or acting according to plan. Since agents are people who put a model into practice just as a subordinate in a hierarchy does, they act in principle in accordance with the instructions and the regulations.

If this legalism slips so easily under the radar, it is because it somehow matches our spontaneous vision of action. In the words of John Dewey, a great philosopher fallen out of fashion but somewhat rehabilitated today, most philosophies are 'spectator philosophies'.[17] The scholastic vision is the vision of a spectator who watches matches, who is not on the pitch, not on the stage, not in the action. This is clearly seen in the relationship with the body. To put it succinctly, there are two ways of looking at the body. There is the one that consists in looking at other people's bodies, or your own body in the mirror, as an object, or the one that consists in being inside, being with, being at one with your body. The scholastic point of view is the point of view of someone who looks at others and has a spectator's philosophy of the body. We can go much further thanks to Maurice

Merleau-Ponty,[18] and this does not mean that we are philosophizing. We are using philosophy to get rid of the philosophy that we indulge in when we don't have a philosophy. We have a philosophy of life, death, existence, the body, being, time, power, and society, which is linked to the fact that we inhabit a scholastic position which supposes a philosophy of the world. This scholastic vision fits us like a glove.

There is therefore in what we are, in our habits of thought, that is to say, in our scholastic bodies, an 'automaton', an implicit philosophy of action as fulfilment of a plan. It has got under our skin. We are happy for others, for the *hoi polloi*, to live according to custom. But we think that for right and proper people, who belong not to the order of the flesh but, as Blaise Pascal says, to the order of the spirit, we cannot talk of custom. Whereas, in fact, the 'thinker' has under their skin, in their brain, in the folds of their thought, that is, in their body, so much that is social. It would be too easy if it were enough to say, 'Look out, take care!' For we have an embodied philosophy, a theory of the subject–object relationship, a theory of reflection (which I demolished at the outset by reminding us that reflection can be an objectification of the reflecting subject), a theory of the body, of time, of history – we even have a philosophy of history which is linked to the scholastic posture, but which becomes modified according to the position we occupy in the scholastic space. Francine Muel-Dreyfus, in her work on educators and primary school teachers,[19] observed that educators had a different philosophy of history from primary school teachers. These are people who, holding different positions in the social space and having reached these positions through different trajectories, had different relationships with the future and therefore different relationships with the past, and thus had a different philosophy of their history, a different way of telling their story in interviews. We have a philosophy of relationships with others which we also draw on when we draft a questionnaire; we have a philosophy of language, a philosophy of what sociology is. Some part of all this is explicit, it's the methodology, it's the epistemological waffle. (I fought in the 1960s to have sociologists discuss epistemology, as an antidote to the positivism that was rampant at the time. Today, epistemology has become the new opium of the sociologists watching themselves think.)

This social history of the social sciences that I would like to try to practise with you is something very difficult. It is, so to speak, the 'art for arts sake' of the profession. One can use the social history of the social sciences, of sociology, to satisfy all sorts of impulses of the un-self-critical academic libido. I'll give you an example: François Dosse's work on structuralism,[20] or the unmediated history, the 'Sciences Po' [official academic] history of intellectuals. This is the main danger: using the apparent objectification that is part of the social history of the social sciences to make a strategic move in the field of the social sciences. To convert an ambition of objectification into a strategic ambition, to convert an ambition of objectification with therapeutic intent – to better understand myself, to better know what I do and what it means to do what I do – into a strategy of cynical self-promotion of the person operating the apparent objectification, who seems to be objectifying. To debunk the 'Dosse effect', we should reread Louis Marin's text on the historiography of the king,[21] the historian's relationship to the king. The historian has a social definition. He is perceived as the *gatekeeper* of posterity. This is why, among the identities that a sociologist can take on, one of the best is historian. If you tell the Banque de France you're a sociologist, you get thrown out; if you say you're a historian, you're fine. The historiographer is someone who passes people into posterity, who canonizes, who eternalizes like a photographer. Like Paul Pellisson for Louis XIV,[22] we can use an appearance of objectification, of historiography, as an instrument for promoting 'historiographed' people. Someone interviews Marcel Gauchet, who is one of the most important agents in the field of social sciences in France, and asks him: 'What do you think of structuralism today?' He answers: 'Structuralism is finished.'

It's a banal strategy in the literary field. In the survey by Jules Huret[23] (a journalist from the *Figaro* who went to interview writers at the end of the last century), all the little Symbolists said: 'Naturalism is finished.' That meant: kill Zola! That's the classic strategy of all young people with regard to the old. In the field of age, the young are unbeatable. They say that the old are old, that they are finished. But celebration has its contradictions. Self-celebration doesn't work very well. If you say, 'I am Napoleon,' you get put away. If you manage to find a third party who will say you are Napoleon, things are looking better already. The longer the chain of celebration, the better it works. If you have a mandated historian, a neutral body, who uses a tape recorder to record for posterity, they have the power of consecration. And what will they consecrate? They will consecrate a position on the spot: Gauchet will tell you that structuralism is finished now, but *sub specie æternitatis*. The same goes for directories. Directories are among the basic objects to be studied by the social history of the social sciences. As long as there have been intellectuals, directories have always been instruments of consecration, of *coups d'état* in a field. The first object of study is these lists: they must be seen not as instruments of knowledge, but as objects to know. The directory of intellectuals, to which a number of people here who have to earn a living have contributed, is one of those objects that are instruments for constructing reality, but can only be used scientifically after a critique of the social conditions of their production.

The sociology of sociology, the history of history, the social history of social history, and the social history of the social sciences are extremely difficult because something that sees itself as a scientific strategy is always revealed to be a strategy in the first degree, a social strategy in the field towards which it apparently adopts a scientific position (a particularly ambitious strategy since it seeks to mount a coup, in the sense of a *coup d'état*, in the field and dress it in the clothing of scientific rationalization). As the sociology of intellectuals has undergone a certain development in France over the last twenty years, the French intellectual field has attained a particularly high degree of distortion in the areas that I am studying. It has become [all the more] difficult to undertake the social history of the social sciences in France, because a certain number of social actors in the fields of cultural production have internalized just enough sociology to be able to make cynical use of it. In other words, the proliferation of directories is motivated by the fact that they are a publishing success, but is also down to the fact that a certain number of people have become aware of the possibilities offered by the 'league table' effect. In scientific struggles, there are more and more people who use the rather imprecise concept of the paradigm: 'my paradigm!' This is a potential object of study for a reflection on the social history of the social sciences, the practical, polemical uses of the social sciences in the struggles within the social sciences.

I would have liked to explain why the notion of field provides some protection against the temptation of the egotistical, pathological (in the Kantian sense[24]) use of sociology or of the social history of the social sciences. Let me take one example: in the 1950s, there were two notorious positions taken by intellectuals. There was

Raymond Aron's book *The Opium of the Intellectuals*, and, confronting it, there was a response to Aron, which was written by Simone de Beauvoir[25] (probably because Jean-Paul Sartre didn't want to do it himself: it's a Kabyle law, you only accept a challenge from a man whose honour is equal to your own). As soon as you have the notion of a field, you ask yourself: where are they located in that space? They are two points of view in space and each sees the other's point of view very well. Simone is very good on Raymond and Raymond is quite good on Simone. This does not mean that the spontaneous point of view from a given point is the truth. The notion of field is an instrument that enables us to break with the tendency to naïvely subscribe to the gaze we project onto a field.

[Inaudible question.]

PB: That's a very good question. How to draft a non-scholastic discourse on the scholastic *habitus*? 'Non-scholastic' meaning something that will waken the scholastics from their scholastic sleep. How to waken them? One way is to sting them with examples. Cartoonists often have instruments of analysis ready to hand. When we intend to demolish a belief, especially a doxic belief, that is to say, a belief that is not formally constituted or clearly expressed, a purely corporeal belief, which people are ready to die for because they feel it in their bones, when we attempt to attack such things as reverence, obedience, or male domination, for instance, the polemical techniques we may use are very important. Thanks to a lot of work, over a number of years, I am able to explain everything that I was trying to find out about myself and my practice since I have been engaged in sociology and ethnology. I try to transmit it through language, because it's my craft, my art, if I have one. [. . .] I try to transmit it not only by saying 'watch me do it', as a ski instructor does; I try to expound some of it explicitly, hoping that, by combining the two, that is, both what I tell you and what you learn in practice by reading articles in *Actes de la recherche en sciences sociales*, by watching people who are going to perform for you, like athletes, I will enable you to acquire what you have come here looking for.

Having said that, I am fully aware that this reflective, explicit, verbalized way is very disappointing. You understand too much and too little. It's too simple, too partial. It took me thirty years to discover that, deep down, dispositions are passions. A boxer has a passion for boxing, they have boxing in their bones and they get their nose broken, but they can't do anything else. It's the same for a mathematician.

It's very difficult to communicate this kind of thing. Because normally you don't communicate it. It's the Zen masters who communicate things like that. I allow myself to say these things. After all, I do it with honourable intentions, not at all with the intention of laying down the law, quite the opposite. For a long time I have been very interested in the pedagogical techniques of the Zen masters. They have similar problems. It's a question of really transforming people. How do you get someone to understand something, *really*? Pascal argues that the automaton must understand.[26] You have all had the experience, when you were practising some sport – you were told: 'Go on, try again,' and you went on to make the same mistake. Because the body hasn't understood. I've interviewed monitors, and music teachers too. How do you get a body to understand what to do? You tell a horn player that they shouldn't blow from the belly, but that they should raise the diaphragm. Well, you would have to be able to talk to the diaphragm! And in sociology, it's the same. All I was saying comes down to this. We have the social in our bones. And yet we want to study the social.

What right do I have to intrude on the intimacy of the individual? I think that insofar as sociology has as its object something that we have just as deeply rooted in the body as what we call bad habits, we need to follow a kind of bodily rehab.

[Inaudible question.]

PB: That's the question you have to ask yourself. What is the intellectual interest? There are two kinds of scientific benefit: you will see how to construct the object, a difficult object, the December movement.[27] If you work on May 1968, on a riot in Bulgaria, and so on, you can transpose. And then, there are interesting aspects of our knowledge of the knowing subject, interests that we could call epistemological. So much for the scientific aspect.

But may the fact that I am interested in this topic today not depend on social determinants that escape me? And although I protest my innocence, am I not in danger of using the social history of the social sciences to defend endangered positions or to impose a form of absolute hegemony, to be a kind of absolute thinker who has thought even the world in which they find themselves. This is possible. All this is linked to my trajectory, to my social position. These are questions that have to be asked. Having said that, I said earlier that reflexivity is not a *cogitatio cogitationis*. But we must add a second thing: the subject of reflexivity is not Bourdieu or X, Y, or Z, it is the field. This is very important. This is what philosophers, who remain confined within a philosophy that is always individual, do not understand. They immediately suspect it of being only an attempt to impose some absolute knowledge. A few years ago, I wrote a text on the great Kantian, Hegelian, and Heideggerian philosophical solutions to the problems of the history of philosophy.[28] Was this not a way of imposing absolute knowledge again, through its sociological variant? This is true only if we consider that the subject of the sociological work is a singular *ego* defined by a proper name. In fact, the field of social sciences is both subject and object of the social history of social sciences. I think that the studies we are about to embark on will raise the self-consciousness of the field to a higher level. The field is going to turn this object of study into an instrument, and a focus of conflict. Everyone will make use of it in order to do battle in the struggles within the field. The instrument, which may have been inspired by a concern to protect the producer of the instrument, can be turned against the author of the instrument. I think that studies like this will by definition unleash criticism, counter-attacks, and polemics. So [it will stimulate] progress, it seems to me, in awareness and knowledge. I deeply believe that the subject of our thoughts is a field. This does not mean that we do not think anything in the first person. We are *habitus* that are largely produced by a field and controlled by a field. One thing follows from what I have just said: I would like you not to be passive, just taking notes. Reflexivity should work collectively. You should be able to intervene, even if only negatively. It will be important for our present collective, strengthened by the awakening consciousness that I hope to arouse, to intervene actively, even if only to say no… That is why I am quite tempted to start with the work of the younger ones among you, because you are the most insecure and vulnerable. That might give you the courage to intervene. At the same time, it can be dangerous for you. I shall think about it. If the procedures that we develop here succeed, they would create the social foundation of a kind of collective reflexive community.

The Cause of Science

How the Social History of the Social Sciences Can Serve the Progress of These Sciences (1995)

The social history of the social sciences is not merely another specialism. It is the privileged instrument of critical reflexivity, an imperative precondition for collective and individual lucidity. No doubt it can [also] fuel resentment and bad faith if exploited merely for the safe satisfactions of retrospective indignation and denunciation, or the guaranteed profits of a risk-free defence of no longer relevant good causes. But it is only truly justified when it succeeds in bringing to light the assumptions which are graven in the very principle of the scientific enterprises of the past and which are perpetuated, often implicitly, by the collective scientific tradition (through its problems, concepts, methods, or techniques).

Only the anamnesis triggered by historical study can deliver us from the amnesia of origins that almost inevitably follows a routine relationship to inherited tradition, translated, for the most part, into the *doxa* of the discipline studied. Such historical study is the only means of providing each researcher with the wherewithal to understand their most fundamental theoretical choices, such as their adherence, most often tacit, to the anthropological theses, which are rarely articulated, but form the basis of their key theoretical and methodological choices (particularly in the philosophy of action), or their epistemological sympathies and antipathies for particular authors, modes of thought, or forms of expression. It is the most indispensable and ruthless instrument for criticizing the passions and interests that are likely to lurk beneath the irreproachable external appearance of the most rigorous methodology.

Social science has the privilege of being able to take its own functioning as an object and to be capable of awakening consciousness to the constraints that weigh on scientific practice. It can therefore make use of consciousness, and of the knowledge it possesses of its functions and its modes of operation, to try to remove some of the obstacles to the progress of consciousness and knowledge. Far from ruining its own foundations [in this way] by condemning it to relativism, as has often been claimed, such a reflexive science can, on the contrary, form the groundwork of a scientific *Realpolitik* aimed at ensuring the progress of scientific reason.

The ambiguous situation of social science

The scientific field is a social microcosm, partially independent of the needs of the macrocosm in which it is embedded. It is, in a sense, a social world *like any other* and, like the economic field, it has its power struggles and its conflicts of interest, coalitions and monopolies, and even its imperialisms and nationalisms. But, whatever the advocates of the 'strong programme' in the sociology of science may say, it is also a *world apart*, with its own laws of operation. All the properties it has in common with other fields take on *specific forms*: for example, however fierce the rivalry between scholars, it remains subject, if not to explicit rules, at least to automatic revisions, such as those resulting from *cross-checking between rivals*, which have the effect of converting social interests such as the appetite for recognition into 'interests of knowledge', converting the *libido dominandi*, which always plays some part in the *libido sciendi*, into the *libido scientifica*, the pure love of truth to which the logic of the field, functioning as an agency of censorship and a principle of sublimation, allocates the objects it judges legitimate and the legitimate ways of apprehending them. The sublimated drives that define this specific *libido* apply to objects that are themselves highly refined and, however violent [they may be], inseparable, in their very existence and in the ways they may be satisfied, from the practical recognition of the demands that are inherent in the social functioning of the field where they may find fulfilment.

It follows that the rigour of scientific products depends fundamentally on the rigour of the specific social constraints that govern their production; or, more precisely, on the degree to which the rules or regularities that govern the scientific microcosm and the conditions under which scientific constructs are produced, communicated, discussed, or criticized are independent of the social world, with its demands, expectations, and requirements.

The field of social sciences is in a very different situation from other scientific fields: because its object is the social world and it claims to produce a scientific representation of it, each of the specialists is in competition not only with other scholars, but also with the professionals of symbolic production (writers, politicians, and journalists) and, in a broader context, with all the social agents who, with very unequal symbolic impact and success, work to impose their vision of the social world (using means ranging from gossip, insult, slander, or calumny to caricatures, pamphlets, or open forums, not to mention institutionalized forms of expression of collective opinion such as voting). This is one of the reasons why [the social scientist] finds it more difficult than other scholars to have their monopoly of the legitimate discourse on their object recognized, when they lay claim to it as a scientist. Their rivals from outside the field, but also sometimes from within, can always appeal to common sense, in opposition to which the scientific representation of the world is built.

They can even appeal to the mode of validating opinion current in politics (especially when the autonomy of the political field tends to be negated by populist demagoguery, that is, pretending to grant everyone the power and the right to judge everything).

Thus, in terms of its degree of autonomy from external powers, public or private, social science is situated halfway between two extremes: on the one hand, the 'purest' scientific fields, such as mathematics, where the producers have no possible clients other than their rivals (who, having the same ability and interest in producing the products themselves, are little inclined to accept others' products without scrutiny); on the other hand, the political or religious fields, or even journalism, where the judgement of specialists is increasingly subject to a verdict by numbers in all its forms (plebiscite, opinion poll, sales figures, or ratings), and where laymen are granted the power to choose between products that they are not necessarily qualified to evaluate (and, even less, to produce).

We are therefore dealing with two completely opposite logics: that of the political field, where the strength of ideas always depends to some extent on the strength of the groups that accept them as true, and that of the scientific field, which, in its purest form, recognizes and acknowledges only the 'intrinsic strength of the true idea', as Baruch Spinoza said: a scientific debate is not settled by a physical confrontation, by a political decision or by a vote, and the strength of an argument depends to a large extent, especially in a highly internationalized field, on proposals or procedures conforming to the rule of logical coherence and factual accuracy. On the contrary, in the political field, the proposals that triumph are those that Aristotle (in *The Topics*[1]) calls the *endoxa* ['reputable beliefs'], that is, those that we have to take into account because the people who count would like them to be true; and also because, as part of the *doxa* of common sense, of our ordinary vision, which is also the most widespread and widely shared, they have the greater number on their side. As such, even when they are completely contrary to logic or experience, these 'leading ideas' can impose themselves because they are backed by the force of a group, and because they are neither true nor even probable, but *plausible* – in the etymological sense of the word –, that is, capable of receiving the approval and applause of the greater number.[2]

The two principles of hierarchization

It follows that, in the field of social sciences as in the field of literature, where the 'pure' and the 'commercial' clash, producers can appeal to one or other of the two [contradictory] principles of hierarchization and legitimization, the scientific principle and the political principle, which confront each other without either managing to impose an exclusive domination. For example, unlike what happens in the most autonomous scientific fields (where no one would think of maintaining today that the earth does not rotate), propositions that are logically inconsistent or incompatible with the facts can be perpetuated and even prosper, as can those who defend them, provided only that they are endowed, both within the field itself and also outside it, with a social authority capable of compensating for their insufficiency or insignificance. The same applies to problems, concepts, or taxonomies: some researchers may, for example, convert *social* problems into *sociological* problems, import into scientific discourse concepts (such as 'profession' or role) or taxonomies (such as individual/collective or 'achievement'/'ascription'[3]) directly from everyday usage and take as instruments of analysis notions that are themselves open to analysis.

We must therefore examine the social obstacles, which are never completely absent, even in the most autonomous scientific fields, that oppose the establishment of the scientific *nomos* as the exclusive criterion for evaluating practices and products. The common root of all these obstacles to scientific autonomy and to the exclusive domination of the scientific principle of evaluation or hierarchization is the set of factors capable of preventing the play of *free scientific competition between peers*, that is, between holders of a basic mastery of the collective discoveries of social science, which is the condition for entry into properly scientific debates; or, in other words, those factors liable to welcome into the game, either as players or as referees (via, for example, a certain type of journalistic criticism), intruders lacking this competence and inclined to introduce extrinsic criteria of production and evaluation, such as those of good sense or 'common sense'.

The conflicts that rack the social sciences (and which are sometimes invoked to deny them the status of sciences) can thus belong to two quite different categories. In the first category, that of strictly scientific conflicts, those who have assimilated the collective discoveries of their science oppose one another according to the inherent logic of problematics and methodology deriving directly from this heritage, which unites them even as they fight to preserve or supersede it. (They are probably never as faithful to their inherited tradition as in their successive breaks with their heritage, whose possibility and necessity are inscribed in the heritage itself.) They confront one another in a disciplined discussion subjecting rigorously *explicated* problems to clearly defined concepts and unambiguous methods of verification. In the second category, that of political conflicts with a scientific dimension, conflicts that are undoubtedly socially inevitable and scientifically analysable, these scientifically trained producers are brought into confrontation with producers who, for various reasons, influenced by, say, age, inadequate training, or ignorance of the minimum requirements of the profession of researcher, lack the appropriate means of production, and by the same token find themselves closer to the expectations of the layman and more capable of satisfying them. (This is the basis of the spontaneous complicity that arises between certain retrograde, outmoded, or ignorant researchers and certain journalists who, unaware of the specific problems, reduce differences in competence to differences in opinion – political or religious, for instance – each tending to make the other seem relative.[4])

Political consensus and scientific conflict

In a properly scientific argument, there is nothing, no object of study, no theory, no fact, that a social taboo should exclude from the discussion, but there is no exclusively social weapon, no argument of authority, no purely academic power even, that is not excluded, in law and in fact, from the universe of means that may be used in the discussion. It follows that, despite appearances, nothing is more alien to this sort of war, which is open to all comers but rigorously regulated in its choice of weapons and legitimate blows, than the *working consensus* of an academic orthodoxy. It was such an orthodoxy that American sociologists in the 1960s and, to a certain extent, the French defenders of the 'New History' tried to establish, relying on what are in fact social powers and first of all on educational establishments, on official publication sites, on professional associations, and even on access to the resources necessary for empirical research.

While we should avoid seeing this as the determining principle of such constructions, the fact remains that the studied ethical and political indifference of a well-bred conservatism, which can be experienced as the 'objective' detachment of the 'impartial observer' or as 'axiological neutrality', is bound to find its identity or fulfilment in theoretical and methodological constructions which are guaranteed to respectfully evoke a gentle, consensual version of the social world and, more generally, in any form of discourse able to use formalism to speak of the social world in a logic of denial, as if it were not speaking of it, or able to use positivism to *be satisfied with* an uncritical recording of the data given.[5]

Thus, American sociologists believed that they had found in the theories of Talcott Parsons or Robert Merton and in the methodology of Paul Lazarsfeld the unified body of doctrine capable of founding the *communis doctorum opinio* of a well-ordered body of 'professionals', *mimicking* what they believed to be the major characteristic of a science worthy of the name: the consensus of the 'scientific community'.[6] In fact, this tacit adherence to the set of undisputed assumptions which underpin the authority of the bodies of doctors, theologians, or jurists, but also, to a certain extent, historians (especially of literature, art, and philosophy, who are hardly inclined to historicize their corpus or its fabrication), is diametrically opposed to the explicit agreement on the objects and issues of disagreement, and on the processes and procedures acceptable for settling differences, that is crucial to the proper functioning of scientific fields.

Indeed, the 'working consensus' of an orthodoxy based on the social complicity of scholars tends to exercise 'social censorship' (disguised as scientific control) either, quite directly, through prohibitions, sometimes explicit, on publication and citation, or, more surreptitiously, through recruitment procedures which exploit networking and 'lobbying' in order to favour social criteria which, more or less successfully disguised as scientific or academic criteria, tend to reserve promotion to positions that encourage production, and thereby scientific competition, for certain categories of agents defined in purely social terms – holders of certain prestigious diplomas, incumbents of certain social positions in teaching or research – or, conversely, to exclude *a priori* certain categories: women, young people, or foreigners, for example.[7]

But while they have undoubtedly contributed greatly to the collapse of orthodoxy, the profound trans-formations that the social sciences have undergone, particularly as a result of the considerable increase in the number of those who practise and study them, have had consequences that are not entirely unambiguous:[8] the *liberating* effects of the emergence of a multitude of competing principles of vision, with the conse-quent intensification of scientific competition, have been matched, in the various national fields, by a strengthening of the factors of heteronomy linked to the increasing dispersion of 'specialists' – which is not very conducive to settling debates between peers – and matched correlatively by a vulnerability to external pressures, solicitations, and injunctions, which, as in all fields, is particularly acute among those most lacking in specific capital.[9]

In short, even though the artificially unified and hierarchical system of the 1950s has given way to a 'polycentric' system, as Howard Becker puts it, and one that is more difficult to supervise because it is fragmented and diversified, the fact remains that, in the United States as in France, the operation of the field is still closer to that of an artistic field in the process of emancipating itself from academic tutelage, where rivals can even deny each other the right to exist, than to that of an advanced scientific field.[10] This is all the more true because, at least in France, social science specialists continue to be bound (particularly through our craving for 'master thinkers') by the literary model of the individual, original 'creator', free from any group or school attachment, and also by the norms of fashion and perpetual renewal within a tradition that govern the field of haute couture and fashion.

Because there are no mechanisms strong enough to impose on the participants a minimum of mutual recognition or, what amounts to the same thing, any obedience to some sort of law governing the waging of war, the confrontation between the different traditions still too often takes the form of an all-out conflict (Randall Collins speaks of 'wars of metatheories') where all means of attack are allowed, from the withering blast of contempt that avoids wasting time on discussion and refutation to the *coups de force* that draw on social powers (such as the suppression of funding or posts, censorship, defamation, or exploiting the influence of the media).

The ambiguous effects of internationalization

What, then, are the mechanisms that could help to ensure that scientific power relations can be established without interference from social power relations? How can we work to abolish or weaken the dualism of the hierarchical principles which, as we have been able to show in the case of France, keeps those researchers most scientifically recognized in the country itself, and especially abroad, away from positions of power over the reproduction of the body of teachers and researchers and, by the same token, over the future of the scientific field and its autonomy?[11] What are the social forces and mechanisms that might form a basis for individual and, above all, collective scientific strategies, with the aim of establishing as a reality that universal confrontation between the researchers best equipped with the most progressive, universal techniques which is the condition for the progress of the universal?

It is undoubtedly from a genuine internationalization of the field of social sciences that we could expect the most effective contribution to the progress of scientific autonomy. Indeed, the pressures of social demand or constraint operate most effectively at the national level, through all the material and symbolic solicitations and incentives that are in play within the national space: since many of the social powers (journalistic, academic, and political, etc.) that confuse or interfere with the scientific struggle exist and persist only on the scale of a nation (the main opposition in all academic-scientific fields is between the 'nationals', who dominate the process of reproduction, and the 'internationals'), most of the spurious oppositions that divide researchers are rooted in local divisions or in local forms of the more general divisions.

That said, the field of the social sciences has always been international, but rarely for the better, and mostly for the worse. First, because even in the purest sciences, where there is a quasi-monopolistic concentration of publication and consecration agencies, the international field can still be a site fostering phenomena of domination, or even specific forms of imperialism. Second, because exchanges – and especially borrowings – tend to follow on from structural homologies shared between the positions occupied in different national fields, that is, almost exclusively between the dominant or between the dominated (resulting, within these two subspaces, in analogous effects of distortion and misunderstanding). There is even every reason to believe that the social obstacles to a *generalized free trade* in scientific ideas may well have been reinforced by a kind of institutionalization of politically based divisions.

In the 1950s, some of the socially dominant sociologists could constitute an invisible international, based on affinities owing more to social than to intellectual motivation and providing the basis for an orthodoxy. Today, as a backlash in the wake of the student movements of the late 1960s and the collective trauma they inflicted on a whole generation of professors from Berkeley to Berlin, the previously informal *connections* have been transformed into networks organized around foundations, journals, and associations, and the well-bred conservatism of the guardians of orthodoxy has given way to the explicit professions of faith and the extremist manifestos of a genuinely reactionary international.[12]

What is new is that there also exists, albeit in a virtual and unco-ordinated state, an international of outsiders made up of all those who have in common their marginal status in relation to the mainstream, such as members of ethnic or sexual minority movements. These 'marginal' people, who are often new entrants, introduce into the field subversive and critical dispositions which, although not always subjected to adequate scientific scrutiny, incline them to break with the routines of the academic establishment. In their struggle against orthodoxy, or what has replaced it, here and there, they often borrow weapons from foreign movements, thus contributing to the internationalization of the social science field;[13] but the interests linked to the position they occupy in the host field are a source of distortion in the selection and perception of the borrowing, which is itself structured according to categories of perception and appreciation linked to a national tradition and, as a result, often quite inadequate. (Because works circulate independently of their context, works conceived in relation to a given space of positions will be received as relating to categories of perception constructed in terms of a completely different space, structured by other proper names, other scholarly -isms, or the same concepts but invested with different meanings, and so forth.)

It follows that, far from automatically contributing to progress towards a higher degree of universalization, the evolution of the international field of social sciences towards a greater unity, particularly through the internationalization of the struggles that it stages, can do no more than contribute to the dissemination on a universal scale (to avoid the particularly treacherous word 'globalization') of spurious antitheses that are profoundly fatal for the progress of science: between quantitative and qualitative methods, between the macro and the micro, between structural and historical approaches, between hermeneutic or internalist visions (the 'text') and externalist visions (the 'context'), between the objectivist vision, often associated with the use of statistics, and the subjectivist, interactionist, or ethnomethodological vision; or, more precisely, between an objectivist structuralism, determined to grasp objective structures through more or less sophisticated quantitative techniques ('path analysis', 'network analysis', etc.) and all the forms of constructivism which, from Herbert Blumer to Harold Garfinkel, via Erving Goffman, have tried to capture, by means of so-called qualitative methods, the representation that agents make of the social world and the contribution that they make to constructing it. This is not to mention the opposition, which takes on a particularly dramatic form in the United States, between an often microscopic 'empiricism', divorced from any fundamental theoretical question, and a 'theory' conceived as a separate specialism and more often than not reduced to a compilation of commentaries on canonical authors or to pedantic 'trend reports' of superficially read and ill-digested works.

If international institutions were really the instrument of scientific rationalization that they could and should be, they should encourage the conduct of an international survey (international at least in its object) of the social determinants (gender, age, social origin, educational career, academic status, specific technical competence, etc.) of the 'choices' between the two terms of the various 'theoretical' and 'methodological' oppositions that present the population of researchers with divisions that are entirely bogus from a scientific point of view. It would undoubtedly show (I am not taking any risks in forwarding this apparently risky hypothesis) that many of these oppositions have no basis other than the social divisions at the heart of the field of social sciences, which themselves express external oppositions, in a more or less refracted form. But I am equally aware that I am not taking a very great risk in predicting that I have very little chance of being heard by those in charge of these bodies: why should they take the trouble to endow with real functions bodies that seem to them sufficiently justified by the fact that they justify their own existence? However, it is reasonable to hope that one day an angry young researcher will take up arms and accept the challenge to reduce to the mundane logic of the passions and interests associated with the various positions in the field the allegedly 'theoretical' or 'epistemological' stances adopted towards the major alternatives of the moment, onto which researchers project, either in direct or inverted form, the shortcomings born of their scientific limitations – as men do onto God, according to Ludwig Feuerbach.

But what makes it difficult (and really risky) to criticize these social antitheses masquerading as epistemological antitheses is the fact that, considered in the light of the principle of social differentiation, the two terms (macro/micro, for example) are most often not on the same level, with one of them always closer to the cause of the dominated (socially and also, very often, scientifically), both within the field (through the social characteristics of its partisans) and, although this is much more difficult to judge, outside the field, so that the purely scientific decision to reject the very principle of the alternative that opposes them may seem to be inspired by a kind of conservative indifference. The fact remains that nothing is more hostile to the progress of an autonomous social science than the temptation of populism: those who believe they are 'serving the cause' of the dominated, which is mainly, in the United States today, the cause of sexual or ethnic minorities, or in France in the 1970s, the 'cause of the people', by abdicating scientific requirements, sometimes in the name of their elitist character or, more naïvely, their link with conservative policies, are not really serving the causes they believe they are defending, which are intimately bound up, at least in the only aspects that matter for a researcher, with the *cause of science*.

The reduction to 'politics' resulting from ignorance of the specific logic of scientific fields implies a renunciation, or in fact a resignation. Reducing the researcher to the role of a simple activist, with no other ends or means than those of an ordinary politician, means negating them as a scholar capable of putting the indispensable weapons of science at the service of the objectives pursued; and above all as a scholar capable of providing the means to understand, among other things, the limits that the social determinants of militant dispositions impose on militant criticism and action (which are too often reduced to simple inversions of dominant positions and, as a result, are too easily reversible – as so many biographical trajectories attest).[14] But above all, we must not shy away from the fact that the reactive, rebellious, or even revolutionary dispositions that some researchers bring into the field, which might be thought to lead inevitably to critical breaks with the *doxa* and orthodoxy, can also encourage submission to external injunctions or constraints, of which the slogans of political movements are only the most visible sign. These dispositions can only engender the genuine break of a *specific revolution* when they are allied with a mastery of the historical achievements of the field (in a very advanced scientific field, the revolutionaries are necessarily endowed with a very specific capital): their awareness and knowledge of the possibilities and impossibilities written into the space of possibilities turn this space both into a system of constraints and sanctions forcing subversive impulses to be sublimated in the form of a scientific break, and into a matrix of all solutions, but only those eligible to be justifiably considered as scientific at a given moment in time.

For a scientific *Realpolitik*

Thus, the questioning of orthodoxies and of all the central principles of vision and division has the indisputable merit of destroying the specious consensus that stifles discussion, but it can lead to a division into antagonistic camps, locked into the metatheoretical conviction of the absolute superiority of their vision – which we cannot accept. We need therefore to work at constructing institutions capable of countering the trend towards anarchic dissolution that is inherent in the multiplicity of modes of thinking, by encouraging a confrontation of points of view inspired by reflexivity.

A point of view that perceives itself as such, that is, as a view taken from a point, a position in a field, is able to overcome its singularity; in particular by partici- pating in a confrontation of different visions based on an awareness of the social determinants of these differences.

But rather than by preaching epistemological wisdom, even informed by a reflexive sociology of the fields of production, it is by transforming the social organization of scientific production and communication and, in particular, the forms of exchange that channel the exercise of logical control that we can expect to found any real progress in scientific reason in the social sciences. It is here that a *Realpolitik* of reason, armed with a rational knowledge of the social mechanisms at work in the field of social sciences, both nationally and internationally, can intervene.

One of the objectives of such a policy may be to strengthen all the mechanisms that contribute to unifying the world's scientific field by promoting scien- tific circulation, to counteract the empire of theoretical or methodological (or, quite simply, linguistic) imperialisms, and, through a systematic appeal to the comparative method (and in particular through a comparative history of the national histories of disciplines), to loosen the grip of national or nation- alistic traditions, most often translated into divisions between theoretical or methodological specialisms and disciplines, or into the problems imposed by the particularities or peculiarities of a necessarily provincial social world.

There are probably no transhistorical universals of communication, whatever Jürgen Habermas may think; but there are certainly socially organized forms of communication that favour the production of the universal. Logic is rooted in a social relation of regulated discussion, based on topics and dialectics. The sites of debate (*topoi*) are a visible manifestation of the problem-solving community reaching the agreement on the grounds of disagreement that is indispensable for discussion (instead of pursuing parallel monologues). This is the kind of playing field that we need to establish, not on the basis of moral prescriptions or proscriptions, but by creating the social conditions for a rational confrontation aiming at establishing on an international scale, not the *working consensus* of an orthodoxy supported by complicity in the interests of those in power, but, if not a rational axiomatic commonwealth, at least a *working dissensus* based on the critical recognition of scientifically (not socially) established compatibilities and incompatibilities. This playing field offers a place for the freedom that social science can win for itself by resolutely applying itself to understanding the social determinants that affect its operations, and by endeavouring to institute the technical processes and social procedures that make it possible to work effectively, that is, *collectively*, to master them.

Bio-bibliographical Markers
Pierre Bourdieu (1930–2002)

1930: Born in Denguin on 1 August (Pyrénées-Atlantiques).

1941–7: Boarder at the Lycée de Pau (Pyrénées-Atlantiques).

1948–51: Boarder at the Lycée Louis-le-Grand in Paris (*hypokhâgne* and *khâgne*) [preparatory classes for the *grandes écoles*]

1951–4: École normale supérieure (ENS).

1954: Obtains the *agrégation* in philosophy.

1954: Teacher at the Lycée de Moulins (Allier).

1955–8: Military service in Algeria.

1958: Assistant at the Faculty of Letters in Algiers; studies of traditional Kabyle society and colonization. *Sociologie de l'Algérie* [*The Algerians,* trans. A. C. M. Ross (Boston: Beacon Press, 1962)].

1960: Statistical survey in collaboration with the Algerian services of the Institute national de statistique et d'études économiques (INSEE) on workers in urban areas. Back in Paris, becomes Raymond Aron's assistant at the Faculté des lettres in Paris.

1961: General Secretary of the Centre de sociologie européenne (CSE), founded and directed by Raymond Aron at the VIth section of the École pratique des hautes études (EPHE); lecturer at the Faculté des lettres in Lille.

1963: *Travail et travailleurs en Algérie*[*].

1964: Elected director of studies at the VIth section of the EPHE; launches the collection 'Le sens commun' at Éditions de Minuit, which he directs until 1992. *Le déracinement. La crise de l'agriculture traditionnelle en Algérie*[*]; *Les héritiers. Les étudiants et la culture*[*] [*The Inheritors: French Students and Their Relation to Culture,*

---

[*] All titles followed by an asterisk were written in collaboration.

trans. Richard Nice (Chicago: University of Chicago Press, 1979)].

1965: *Un art moyen. Essai sur les usages sociaux de la photographie*[*] [*Photography: A Middle-brow Art*, trans. Shaun Whiteside (Cambridge: Polity, 1990)]; *Rapport pédagogique et communication*[*].

1966: *L'amour de l'art. Les musées et leur public*[*]; [*The Love of Art: European Art Museums and Their Public*, trans. W. C. Beattie and N. Merriman (Cambridge: Polity, 1990)]; *Le partage des bénéfices. Expansion et inégalités en France*[*].

1968: *Le métier de sociologue. Préalables épistémologiques*[*] [*The Craft of Sociology: Epistemological Preliminaries*, trans. Richard Nice, ed. Beate Kreis (New York: Walter de Gruyter, 1991)].

1969: Creation of the Centre de sociologie de l'éducation et de la culture du Centre de sociologie européenne (CSEC-CSE, an autonomous team originally from the CSE, recognized as an independent unit in 1970).

1970: *La reproduction. Éléments pour une théorie du système d'enseignement*[*] [*Reproduction in Education, Society and Culture*, trans. Richard Nice (London: SAGE, 1977)].

1972: Visiting Fellow at the Institute for Advanced Study in Princeton for one year. *Esquisse d'une théorie de la pratique* [*Outline of a Theory of Practice*, trans. Richard Nice (Cambridge: Cambridge University Press, 1977)].

1974: Member of the American Academy of Arts and Sciences (Cambridge, MA).

1975: Launch of the journal *Actes de la recherche en sciences sociales*, which he directed until his death.

1977: *Algérie 60. Structures économiques et structures temporelles* [*Algeria 1960,* trans. Richard Nice (Cambridge: Cambridge University Press, 1979)].

1979: *La distinction. Critique sociale du jugement* [*Distinction: A Social Critique of the Judgement of Taste*, trans. Richard Nice (Abingdon: Routledge, 1984)].

1980: *Le sens pratique* [*The Logic of Practice*, trans. Richard Nice (Cambridge: Polity, 1990)]; *Questions de sociologie* [*Sociology in Question*, trans. Richard Nice (London: SAGE, 1993)].

1981: Elected to the Collège de France as professor of sociology.

1982: Inaugural lecture at the Collège de France on 23 April. *Leçon sur la leçon* ['A Lecture on the Lecture', in *In Other Words: Essays Towards a Reflexive Sociology*, trans. Matthew Adamson (Cambridge: Polity, 1990), pp. 177–98]; *Ce que parler veut dire. L'économie des échanges linguistiques* ['The Economy of Linguistic Exchanges', in *Language and Symbolic Power*, trans. Gino Raymond and Matthew Adamson, ed. John B. Thompson (Cambridge: Polity, 1991), pp. 35–102].

1984: *Homo academicus* [*Homo Academicus*, trans. Peter Collier (Cambridge: Polity, 1988)].

1985: CSE is associated with the Collège de France; honorary doctorate from the Free University of Berlin. *Propositions pour l'enseignement de l'avenir (élaborées à la demande de Monsieur le Président de la République par les professeurs du Collège de France)** ['Proposals for the Future of Education', in *Political Interventions: Social Science and Political Action*, trans. David Fernbach (London: Verso, 2008 [2002]), pp. 156–9].

1987: *Choses dites* [*In Other Words* – see 1982].

1988: *L'ontologie politique de Martin Heidegger* [*The Political Ontology of Martin Heidegger*, trans. Peter Collier (Cambridge: Polity, 1991)].

1989: Launch of the review *Liber* in collaboration with several European newspapers. *Principes pour une réflexion sur les contenus de l'enseignement**, report of the commission chaired by Pierre Bourdieu and François Gros, ministère de l'Éducation nationale, de la Jeunesse et des Sports [*Principles for Reflecting on the Curriculum*, report of the commission chaired by Pierre Bourdieu and François Gros, Ministry of National Education, Youth, and Sports, in Anne Corbett and Bob Moon (eds), *Education in France: Continuity and Change in the Mitterrand Years, 1981–1985* (London: Routledge, 1996), pp. 327–34]; *La noblesse d'État. Grandes écoles et esprit de corps* [*The State Nobility: Elite Schools in the Field of Power*, trans. Lauretta C. Clough (Cambridge: Polity, 1996)].

1992: *Réponses. Pour une anthropologie réflexive** [*An Invitation to Reflexive Sociology* (Cambridge: Polity, 1992)]; *Les règles de l'art. Genèse et structure du champ littéraire* [*The Rules of Art: Genesis and Structure of the Literary Field*, trans. Susan Emanuel (Cambridge: Polity, 1996)].

1993: Gold medal of the Centre national de la recherche scientifique (CNRS); member of the Academia Europaea (Cambridge, UK). *La misère du monde** [*The Weight of the World: Social Suffering in Contemporary Society*, trans. Priscilla Parkhurst Ferguson et al. (Cambridge: Polity, 1999)].

1994: *Liber* becomes *Revue internationale des livres. Libre échange**; *Raisons pratiques. Sur la théorie de l'action*

[*Practical Reason: On the Theory of Action*, trans. Randal Johnson et al. (Cambridge: Polity, 1998)].

1995: Commitment to the social protest movement of December 1995.

1996: Honorary doctorate from the Johann Wolfgang Goethe University in Frankfurt and the University of Athens; Erving Goffman Prize from the University of California at Berkeley; creation of the Liber-Raisons d'agir publishing house and the Raisons d'agir collective. *Sur la télévision* [*On Television and Journalism*, trans. Priscilla Parkhurst Ferguson (London: Pluto Press, 1998)].

1997: Creation of the 'Liber' collection at Éditions du Seuil; awarded the Ernst Bloch Prize by the city of Ludwigshafen (Germany). *Méditations pascaliennes* [*Pascalian Meditations*, trans. Richard Nice (Cambridge: Polity, 2000)]; *Les usages sociaux de la science. Pour une sociologique clinique du champ scientifique.*

1998: Last publication of *Liber. Revue Internationale des livres*; *Contre-feux. Propos pour servir à la résistance contre l'invasion néo-libérale* [*Acts of Resistance: Against the New Myths of Our Times*, trans. Richard Nice (Cambridge: Polity, 1998)]; *La domination masculine* [*Male Domination*, trans. Richard Nice (Cambridge: Polity, 2001)].

1999: Honorary doctorate from the University of Joensuu (Finland).

2000: Huxley Memorial Medal of the Royal Anthropological Institute of Great Britain and Ireland. *Propos sur le champ politique*; *Les structures sociales de l'économie* [*The Social Structure of the Economy*, trans. Chris Turner (Cambridge: Polity, 2005)].

2001: *Contre-feux 2. Pour un mouvement social européen* [*Firing Back: Against the Tyranny of the Market*, trans. Loïc Wacquant (New York: The New Press, 2003)]; *Langage et pouvoir symbolique* [*Language and Symbolic Power* – see 1982]; *Science de la science et réflexivité. Cours du Collège de France (2000–2001)*; [*Science of Science and Reflexivity*, trans. Richard Nice (Cambridge: Polity, 2004)].

2002: Dies on 23 January. *Le bal des célibataires. Crise de la société paysanne en Béarn* [*The Bachelors' Ball: The Crisis of Peasant Society in Béarn*, trans. Richard Nice (Cambridge: Polity, 2008)]; *Interventions (1961–2001)* [*Political Interventions* – see 1985]. *Si le monde social m'est supportable, c'est parce que je peux m'indigner*[*].

2003: *Images d'Algérie. Une affinité élective* [*Picturing Algeria*, eds Franz Schultheis and Christine Frisinghelli (New York: Columbia University Press, 2012)].

2004: *Esquisse pour une auto-analyse* [*Sketch for a Self-Analysis*, trans. Richard Nice (Cambridge: Polity, 2007)].

2008: *Esquisses algériennes* [*Algerian Sketches*, trans. David Fernbach (Cambridge: Polity, 2013)]; *La production de l'idéologie dominante**.

2010: *Le sociologue et l'historien**.

2012: *Sur l'État. Cours au Collège de France (1989–1992)* [*On the State: Lectures at the Collège de France (1989–1992)*, trans. David Fernbach (Cambridge: Polity, 2014)].

2013: *Manet, une révolution symbolique. Cours au Collège de France (1998–2000)* [*Manet: A Symbolic Revolution. Lectures at the Collège de France (1998–2000)*, trans. Peter Collier and Margaret Rigaud-Drayton (Cambridge: Polity, 2017)].

2014: *Invitation à la sociologie réflexive** [*An Invitation to Reflexive Sociology* – see 1992].

2015–16: *Sociologie générale. Cours au Collège de France (1981–1986)*, 2 vols [*General Sociology: Lectures at the Collège de France (1981–1986)*, 5 vols, trans. Peter Collier (Cambridge: Polity, 2018–23): *Classification Struggles*, 2018; *Habitus and Field*, 2020; *Forms of*

Capital, 2021; *Principles of Vision*, 2022; *Politics and Sociology*, 2023]; *Anthropologie économique. Cours au Collège de France (1992–1993)*; *La force du droit. Éléments pour une sociologie du champ juridique.*

2022: *L'intérêt au désintéressement* [*The Interest of Disinterestedness*, trans. Peter Collier (Cambridge: Polity, 2024)]; *Microcosmes. Théorie des champs.*

Notes

Introduction: From Epistemological Vigilance to Reflexivity

1 Afterwards, Bourdieu's career took place mainly in the VIth section of the École pratique des hautes études (EPHE), which became the École des hautes études en sciences sociales (EHESS), to which the CSE is attached. Bourdieu was elected director of studies there in 1964, became the director of the CSE in 1969, and retained joint membership of the EHESS after his election to the Collège de France in 1981.

2 Pierre Bourdieu, *Sketch for a Self-Analysis*, trans. Richard Nice (Cambridge: Polity, 2007 [2004]), p. 51.

3 Pierre Bourdieu, *Travail et travailleurs en Algérie*, ed. Amín Pérez and Tassadit Yacine (Paris: Raisons d'agir, 2021 [1963]), especially the introduction, 'Statistiques et sociologie', and the foreword, 'Les conditions d'une science sociale décoloniale' (pp. 19–29 and 31–47). The book is the result of a collaborative project with three

statisticians from the Institut national de la statistique et des études économiques (INSEE), Alain Darbel, Jean-Paul Rivet, and Claude Seibel; the reprint does not contain the statistical part.

4 Pierre Bourdieu, *The Bachelors' Ball*, trans. Richard Nice (Cambridge: Polity, 2007 [2002]).

5 Bourdieu, *Sketch for a Self-Analysis*, p. 59.

6 Ibid., pp. 59–60.

7 Pierre Bourdieu, Jean-Claude Chamboredon, and Jean-Claude Passeron, *The Craft of Sociology: Epistemological Preliminaries*, trans. Richard Nice, ed. Beate Kreis (New York: de Gruyter, 1991 [1968]), pp. 72–7.

8 Yves Gingras, 'Réflexivité et sociologie de la connaissance scientifique', in Louis Pinto, Gisèle Sapiro, and Patrick Champagne (eds), *Pierre Bourdieu, sociologue* (Paris: Fayard, 2004), pp. 337–47.

9 Pierre Bourdieu, *Pascalian Meditations*, trans. Richard Nice (Cambridge: Polity, 2000 [1997]), p. 10.

10 On the three levels of objectification, see Pierre Bourdieu, *Science of Science and Reflexivity*, trans. Richard Nice (Cambridge: Polity, 2004 [2001]), p. 94.

11 For these examples, see Bourdieu, *Travail et travailleurs en Algérie*, pp. 36–40.

12 Pierre Bourdieu, 'L'objectivation participante', *Actes de la recherche en sciences sociales*, no. 150, 2003, pp. 43–58.

13 Ibid., p. 51.

14 Pierre Bourdieu, 'Secouez un peu vos structures!', in Jacques Dubois, Pascal Durand, and Yves Winkin (eds), *Le symbolique et le social. La réception internationale de la*

pensée de Pierre Bourdieu (Liège: Presses Universitaires de Liège, 2005), pp. 325–41, here pp. 336–7.

15 Bourdieu, *Science of Science and Reflexivity*, p. 89.

16 The CNJS was created in 1965 by 'young researchers in the exact sciences, influenced by Marxism, [who] were considering the possibility of committing themselves to the left as researchers, without following the scientistic model of their elders' (Mathieu Quet, 'L'innovation éditoriale des revues de critique des sciences', *Médiamorphoses*, special issue '68 et les médias, quarante ans après', April 2008, pp. 225–30, here p. 226).

17 'Science Policy' was one of the four programmes of the CSE at the time, the others being Culture and Education, Senior Administration, and Economic Sociology: CSE, *Rapport d'activité 1966–1967. Programme de travail 1967–1968* (Paris: CSE Archives, 1 July 1967 [typescript]).

18 Luc Boltanski and Pascale Maldidier, *La vulgaris-ation scientifique et ses agents* (Paris: CSE, 1969 [typescript]); Luc Boltanski and Pascale Maldidier, 'Carrière scientifique, morale scientifique, et vulgaris-ation', *Information sur les sciences sociales*, vol. 9, no. 3, 1970, pp. 99–118.

19 The journal (ten volumes published from 1966 to 1969), published by the 'Cercle d'épistémologie de l'École normale supérieure', is available online at http://cahiers. kingston.ac.uk/.

20 Pierre Bourdieu and Jean-Claude Passeron, 'Sociology and Philosophy in France since 1945: Death and

Resurrection of a Philosophy without Subject', *Social Research*, vol. 34, no. 1, 1967, pp. 162–212.

21 Bourdieu et al., *The Craft of Sociology*, p. 51.

22 Pierre Bourdieu, *Outline of a Theory of Practice*, trans. Richard Nice (Cambridge: Cambridge University Press,1977 [1972]), p. vii.

23 This text has had different versions: 'La spécificité du champ scientifique et les conditions sociales du progrès de la raison', *Sociologie et sociétés*, vol. 7, no. 1, 1975, pp. 91–118; 'Le champ scientifique', *Actes de la recherche en sciences sociales*, nos 2–3, 1976, pp. 88–104; and, the most recent version, 'L'histoire singulière de la raison scientifique', *Zilsel*, no. 4, 2018, pp. 281–319. (On the history of this text, see the contribution by Jérôme Lamy and Arnaud Saint-Martin, 'La raison a une histoire', ibid., pp. 273–80.)

24 Pierre Bourdieu, *Sociologie générale*, vol. 1, *Cours au Collège de France, 1981–1983*, ed. Patrick Champagne et al. (Paris: Raisons d'agir, 2015), p. 15.

25 Pierre Bourdieu and Loïc J. D. Wacquant, *An Invitation to Reflexive Sociology* (Cambridge: Polity, 1992), p. 63 [translation adjusted here].

26 On these developments, see Yves Gingras, 'Un air de radicalisme. Sur quelques tendances récentes en sociologie de la science et de la technologie', *Actes de la recherche en sciences sociales*, no. 108, 1995, pp. 3–17; Bourdieu, *Science of Science and Reflexivity*, p. 1; Jacques Bouveresse, *Prodiges et vertiges de l'analogie. De l'abus des belles-lettres dans la pensée* (Paris: Raisons d'agir, 1999).

On the sociology of science, see Terry Shinn and Pascal Ragouet, *Controverses sur la science. Pour une sociologie transversaliste de l'activité scientifique* (Paris: Raisons d'agir, 2005); Yves Gingras, *Sociologie des sciences* (Paris: Presses universitaires de France, 2013).

27 On the pedagogy of research, see Pierre Bourdieu, 'Handing Down a Trade', in Bourdieu and Wacquant, *An Invitation to Reflexive Sociology*, pp. 218–24.

28 Thematic issues: 'Histoire sociale des sciences sociales', *Actes de la recherche en sciences sociales*, nos 106–7 and no. 108, 1995.

Epistemology and the Sociology of Sociology (1967)

1 Pierre Gréco (1927–88), a graduate of the École normale supérieure, was Jean Piaget's assistant during his lecture courses on psychology at the Sorbonne between 1952 and 1962. He participated in the research at Piaget's Centre international d'épistémologie génétique (1955–85) in Geneva, and from the mid-1960s devoted himself to teaching at the VIth section of the École pratique des hautes études (EPHE). There he was secretary of the Enseignement préparatoire à la recherche approfondie en sciences sociales (EPRASS) programme, in which Pierre Bourdieu and Jean-Claude Passeron participated and which constituted the main context for the writing of *The Craft of Sociology* (1968).

2 Gaston Bachelard, *Le rationalisme appliqué* (Paris: Presses universitaires de France, 1949), pp. 4–11.

3 The 'cargo cult' is a set of beliefs and rituals first observed

by ethnologists among the Melanesian Aborigines which involves imitating American and Japanese radio operators ordering supplies, in the hope of receiving cargo ships filled with Western goods.

4 'A new experiment may lead to a fundamental change in scientific thinking. In science, any "discourse on method" can only be provisional [. . .]' (Gaston Bachelard, *The New Scientific Spirit*, trans. Arthur Goldhammer, Boston: Beacon Press, 1984 [1934], p. 136).

Narcissistic Relexivity and Scientific Reflexivity (1993)

1 Wes Sharrock and Bob Anderson, *The Ethnomethodologists* (Chichester: Ellis Horwood Press/London: Tavistock, 1986), pp. 35 and 106.

2 Alvin W. Gouldner, *The Coming Crisis of Western Sociology* (New York: Basic Books, 1970).

3 Clifford Geertz, *Works and Lives: The Anthropologist as Author* (Stanford: Stanford University Press, 1988), p. 89.

4 George E. Marcus and Michael M. J. Fischer, *Anthropology as Cultural Critique: An Experimental Moment in the Human Sciences* (Chicago: The University of Chicago Press, 1986); Renato Rosaldo, *Culture and Truth: The Remaking of Social Analysis* (Boston: Beacon Press, 1989).

5 James Clifford and George E. Marcus (eds), *Writing Culture: The Poetics and Politics of Ethnography* (Berkeley: University of California Press, 1986).

6 Steve Woolgar, 'Reflexivity is the Ethnographer of the Text', in Steve Woolgar (ed.), *Knowledge and Reflexivity: New Frontiers in the Sociology of Knowledge* (London: SAGE Publications, 1988), pp. 14–34, here p. 14.

7   Émile Durkheim, *The Rules of Sociological Method*, trans. W. D. Halls (New York: The Free Press, 1982 [1895]).

8   Pierre Bourdieu, Jean-Claude Chamboredon, and Jean-Claude Passeron, *The Craft of Sociology*, trans. Richard Nice, ed. Beate Kreis (New York: de Gruyter, 1991 [1968]).

9   Pierre Bourdieu, *Homo Academicus*, trans. Peter Collier (Cambridge: Polity, 1989 [1984]).

10 Reference to the short passage on the 'scholastic view' in John L. Austin, *Sense and Sensibilia*, ed. Geoffrey J. Warnock (London: Oxford University Press, 1962), pp. 2–4.

11 Ludwig Wittgenstein, 'Remarks on Frazer's *The Golden Bough*', in *The Mythology in Our Language: Remarks on Frazer's Golden Bough*, trans. Stephen Palmié, ed. Giovanni da Col and Stephen Palmié (Chicago: HAU Books, 2018), pp. 29–73.

12 On these forms of epistemocentrism, see Pierre Bourdieu, *Pascalian Meditations*, trans. Richard Nice (Cambridge: Polity, 2000 [1997]), pp. 50–4.

Proposal for a Social History of the Social Sciences (1997)

1   Pierre Bourdieu and Loïc J. D. Wacquant, *An Invitation to Reflexive Sociology* (Cambridge: Polity, 1992).

2   Bourdieu develops the second 'type of profit' later in the text (see pp. 57–8).

3   Pierre Bourdieu (ed.), *The Weight of the World: Social Suffering in Contemporary Society*, trans. Priscilla Parkhurst Ferguson et al. (Cambridge: Polity, 1990).

4   On the effects of Delacroix's and Duchamp's relatively

high level of education, see Pierre Bourdieu, *General Sociology: Lectures at the Collège de France (1981–1986)*, Vol. 4: *Principles of Vision*, trans. Peter Collier (Cambridge: Polity, 2022 [2016]), pp. 60–1.

5 In his opposition to the classical academic style, Martin Heidegger often refers to Friedrich Hölderlin and his *Begriffsdichtung*, his conceptual poetry (Pierre Bourdieu, *The Political Ontology of Martin Heidegger*, trans. Peter Collier, Cambridge: Polity, 1991, pp. 54, 100).

6 Pierre Bourdieu, *The Logic of Practice*, trans. Richard Nice (Cambridge: Polity, 1990), p. 163.

7 John L. Austin, *Sense and Sensibilia*, ed. Geoffrey J. Warnock (London: Oxford University Press, 1962), p. 3.

8 Pierre Bourdieu, 'Bachelorhood and the Peasant Condition' (1962), in *The Bachelors' Ball: The Crisis of Peasant Society in Béarn*, trans. Richard Nice (Cambridge: Polity, 2008), pp. 7–130. This study was carried out in 1959–60 in a village in Béarn.

9 Pierre Bourdieu, *Homo Academicus*, trans. Peter Collier (Cambridge: Polity, 1988 [1984]).

10 Plato, *Theaetetus* 190, in *The Dialogues of Plato Translated into English with Analyses and Introductions*, Vol. 2, trans. Benjamin Jowett (Oxford: Clarendon Press, 1942), p. 193 (trans. note).

11 Pierre Bourdieu, 'Questions de politique', *Actes de la recherche en sciences sociales*, no. 16, 1977, pp. 55–89.

12 Gary S. Becker, *Human Capital: A Theoretical and Empirical Analysis, with Special Reference to Education* (New York: National Bureau of Economic Research, 1964). For a critical discussion of this notion, see Pierre

Bourdieu, *General Sociology: Lectures at the Collège de France (1981–1986)*, Vol. 3: *Forms of Capital*, trans. Peter Collier (Cambridge: Polity, 2021), pp. 162–6.

13 See note 9 above.

14 Bourdieu, 'Bachelorhood and the Peasant Condition'.

15 See, in the thematic issue 'La critique du discours lettré', Bourdieu's articles entitled 'La lecture de Marx, ou quelques remarques critiques à propos de "Quelques remarques critiques à propos de *Lire le capital*"' and 'L'ontologie politique de Martin Heidegger' (*Actes de la recherche en sciences sociales*, nos 5–6, 1975, pp. 65–79 and 109–56, respectively). Under the title 'Le discours d'importance', the first text is reprinted in *Ce que parler veut dire* (Paris: Fayard, 1982), pp. 207–26; the second text gave rise to the book on Heidegger of the same title (*The Political Ontology of Martin Heidegger*).

16 Claude Lévi-Strauss, *The Elementary Structures of Kinship*, trans. James Harle Bell and John Richard von Sturmer, ed. Rodney Needham (Boston: Beacon Press, 1971 [1947]). Bourdieu's theory of practice breaks with the tendency of ethnologists to understand observable regularities as the product of obedience to 'rules' or the result of the unconscious regulation of a cerebral or social mechanism (Pierre Bourdieu, *Outline of a Theory of Practice*, trans. Richard Nice, Cambridge: Cambridge University Press, 1977 [1972], pp. 22–30).

17 John Dewey, *The Later Works, 1925–1953*, Vol. 4: *1929: The Quest for Certainty*, ed. Jo Ann Boydston (Carbondale: Southern Illinois University Press, 1984 [1929]), p. 19.

18 Maurice Merleau-Ponty, *The Structure of Behaviour*, trans. Alden L. Fisher (Pittsburgh: Duquesne University Press, 1983 [1942]); *Phenomenology of Perception*, trans. Donald A. Landes (London: Routledge, 2013 [1945]).

19 Francine Muel-Dreyfus, *Le métier d'éducateur. Les instituteurs de 1900, les éducateurs spécialisés de 1968* (Paris: Minuit, 1983).

20 François Dosse, *Histoire du structuralisme*, Vol. 1: *Le champ du signe, 1945–1966*, Vol. 2: *Le chant du cygne, de 1967 à nos jours* (Paris: La Découverte, 1991 and 1992); François Dosse, *Des Annales à la 'nouvelle histoire'* (Paris: La Découverte, 1987).

21 Louis Marin, *Le portrait du roi* (Paris: Minuit, 1981).

22 Paul Pellisson (1624–93), historiographer of Louis XIV, quoted in ibid.

23 Jules Huret, *Enquête sur l'évolution littéraire*, notes and preface by by Daniel Grojnowski (Vanves: Thot, 1982).

24 Kant uses the term to mean 'dependent upon sensibility' (trans. note).

25 Raymond Aron, *The Opium of the Intellectuals* (Piscataway, NJ: Transaction, 2001 [1955]); Simone de Beauvoir, 'Right-wing Thought Today' (1955), in *Political Writings* (Champaign: University of Illinois Press, 2012), pp. 103–94.

26 'Custom is for us the strongest and most readily accepted proof: it sways the automaton, which bears the unthinking mind along with it' (Blaise Pascal, *Pensées*, trans. John Warrington [London: Dent, 1960], p. 2).

27 A reference to the social movement of December 1995

which assembled more than a million people against the 'neoliberal' reforms of Alain Juppé's government. Bourdieu committed himself to the movement, which deeply divided the intellectuals: Pierre Bourdieu, *Political Interventions: Social Science and Political Action*, trans. David Fernbach (London: Verso, 2008 [2002]), pp. 271–313; Julien Duval et al., *Le 'décembre' des intellectuels français* (Paris: Raisons d'agir, 2000).

28 Pierre Bourdieu, 'Les sciences sociales et la philosophie', *Actes de la recherche en sciences sociales*, nos 47–8, 1983, pp. 45–52.

The Cause of Science: How the Social History of the Social Sciences Can Serve the Progress of These Sciences (1995)

1 Aristotle, *The Organon*, Vol. 5: *Topics*, trans. W. A. Pickard (Scotts Valley, CA: Createspace, 2012) (ed. note).

2 The ambiguity of certain public discussions with scientific ambitions is suddenly revealed when the public drops the passive role usually assigned to it to show its approval of one or other of the debaters by more or less sustained applause; and the violence of the tyrannical – in Pascal's sense – intrusion of the laymen erupts when one of the participants resorts to the rhetorical device that Arthur Schopenhauer considered typically perfidious, and which consists in addressing an argument to his opponent to which the latter could only respond by using arguments that are incomprehensible to the audience.

3 Used by the sociologist Talcott Parsons to distinguish the

acquisition of a social position by the agent's own effort (*achievement*) or by social attribution (*ascription*) (ed. note).

4 The two principles of differentiation are not completely independent: conformist dispositions, which tend to accept the world as it is, or reactive or rebellious dispositions, which tend to resist social constraints, both internal and above all external, and to break with the most widely shared evidence within and outside the field, are undoubtedly not randomly distributed among the occupants of the different positions in the field and among the trajectories they have followed to reach them.

5 It could be shown that neoclassical economics has some of the major characteristics of an orthodoxy *mimicking* scientificity (with the very special efficiency conferred by mathematical formalization), such as the tacit acceptance of unchallenged assumptions on very fundamental points (in the theory of action, for example).

6 The theory of professions as expressed in the article under this title by Talcott Parsons for the *International Encyclopedia of the Social Sciences* (David L. Sills, ed., New York: Macmillan, 1968, pp. 536–46) can be read as the professional pledge of the 'professionals', which is how the establishment sociologists intend to be seen. These professionals, characterized, according to Parsons, by their intellectual training and an authority based more on expertise than on political power, these professionals are free from any dependence on the state and government bureaucracy and are guided by the sole concern for the *common good*. This 'collectivity-orientation', this 'selflessness' and 'altruism', which can

ensure the highest material and symbolic rewards, and which is mentioned in most definitions of the professions, can also be found in Robert Merton's representation of the scientific universe. In short, the pre-constructed notion of 'profession', a conceptual 'readymade' that has given rise to countless comments and criticism, is less a description of a social reality than a practical contribution to the construction of sociology as a 'profession', and a scientific one.

7 Since we cannot give examples from the French field today (those who, in the name of liberalism, indulge in practices worthy of the most authoritarian regimes would no doubt be the first to denounce as 'totalitarian' any denunciation of such practices), we should quote here the entire passage from the famous lecture on 'Science as a Vocation', in which Max Weber asks the question, usually reserved for private conversations, of why universities and research institutions do not always select the best: dismissing the temptation to blame 'personal shortcomings in either faculties or the Ministries of Education', for the fact that 'so many mediocrities occupy leading positions in our universities', he invites us to seek the reasons for this state of affairs 'in the laws governing human cooperation', those which, in the election of popes or American presidents, almost always lead to the selection of 'the second or third candidate on the list', and he concludes, not without irony: 'What is astonishing is not that mistakes are often made, but that, despite everything, the number of *good* appointments is relatively large' (Max Weber, 'Science as a Vocation', in *The Vocation Lectures*, trans. Rodney Livingstone, Indianapolis: Hackett, 2004, pp. 4–5).

8   Howard S. Becker, in a chapter entitled 'What's Happening to Sociology?' in his book *Doing Things Together* (Evanston, IL: Northwestern University Press, 1986, p. 209), observes that the number of sociologists listed by the American Sociological Association rose from 2,364 in 1950 to 15,567 in 1978. Similarly, in France, the number of sociologists in the same period rose from 200 to about 1,000 (the Association des Sociologues, which adopts a very broad definition, lists 1,678 public and private sociologists). To be more precise, in 1949, the Centre national de la recherche scientifique (CNRS) had only 18 sociologists; in 1967, there were 112, 135 at the École pratique des hautes études (EPHE) and 290 in the research centres, that is, more than 500 in all; in 1980, there were 261 sociologists at the CNRS alone.

9   Morphological changes resulting from the abolition of the *numerus clausus*, *de facto* or *de jure*, which protects a body by guaranteeing the *scarcity* of its members, are very often the direct cause of transformations in the fields of cultural production: they are, in any case, the specific mediation through which the effects of economic and social changes are exercised. Moreover, the form and intensity of these changes and the effects they produce depend on the state of the structure of the field in which they occur. For this reason, we should reject as a typical example of the short-circuit error the explanation that relates changes in a specialized field such as sociology directly to global transformations, such as post-war prosperity (Norbert Wiley, 'The Current Interregnum in American Sociology', *Social Research*, vol. 52, no. 1, 1985, pp. 179–207, especially p. 185), or to the changes in

sociology and history, both in France and in Germany, in the 1970s, with the transformations of the political mood around 1968, which are themselves linked to morphological changes in the specialized fields of production and to intellectual innovations favoured or authorized by the effects of these changes.

10 'Quantitativist sociologists speak with pride of their "mathematical revolution" and their attainment of high levels of sophistication in statistical techniques, and they sometimes dismiss the rest of the field rather scornfully as a small and meaningless nonquantitativist minority. Marxist sociologists, with the confidence that goes with no longer being confned to the underground, dismiss "positivism" as the ideological reflection of an outdated historical epoch. Historical sociologists (who may also be Marxists) argue for the uniqueness of historical patterns and the need to ground everything in its real place in very specific historical sequences. Ethnomethodologists dismiss the sociology of the macro world as an unjustifiable gloss; a variety of phenomenological, humanistic Parisian structuralist and other positions prove with philosophical sophistication (and a good deal of contempt for their philosophically illiterate opponents) that only their methods provide any adequate grasp of the social world at all' (Randall Collins, 'Is 1980s Sociology in the Doldrums?', *American Journal of Sociology*, vol. 91, no. 6, 1986, pp. 1336–55, here. p. 1341).

11 Pierre Bourdieu, *Homo Academicus*, trans. Peter Collier (Cambridge: Polity, 1988 [1984]).

12 These networks are the basis for exchanges of services (invitations, reports, funding), which mean, for example, that the use of international peer reviewers, particularly in co-option procedures, is not always a guarantee of universality.

13 Generally speaking, the best weapons for internal conflicts in national fields are those imported, especially when it is a question of *discrediting* an established position or accrediting a new position and accelerating the always difficult process of initial accumulation, that is, of subverting the reigning social hierarchy and imposing new rules for establishing values. (We know, for example, the polemical use that real or supposed 'cosmopolitans' can make of the idea of national 'backwardness'.)

14 It is remarkable that Michel Foucault, who, at least in the United States, has become the ritually invoked patron saint (more than the master thinker) of all subversive movements, should be subjected to such a reduction by the preachers of restoration (see James Miller, *The Passion of Michel Foucault*, New York: Simon & Schuster, 1993; and Didier Eribon's critique of it, *Michel Foucault et ses contemporains*, Paris: Fayard, 1994, pp. 22–30). But by reducing all of Foucault's thought to his homosexuality, they only reverse the position of those who intend to canonize him because he was homosexual (see David Halperin, *Saint Foucault: Two Essays in Gay Hagiography*, Oxford: Oxford University Press, 1995).